POTIONS, ELIXIRS & BREWS

ANAÏS ALEXANDRE

WATKINS
Sharing Wisdom Since 1893

POTIONS, ELIXIRS & BREWS
ANAÏS ALEXANDRE

First published in the UK and USA in 2020
by Watkins Media Limited
Unit 11, Shepperton House, 83–93
Shepperton Road
London N1 3DF

enquiries@watkinspublishing.com

Commissioning Editor: Ella Chappell
Managing Designer: Francesca Corsini
Production: Uzma Taj
Commissioned artwork: Lolle (Lorenza Scarsi)
loll3.tumblr.com

A CIP record for this book is available from
the British Library

ISBN: 978-1-78678-434-6 (Hardback)
ISBN: 978-1-78678-450-6 (eBook)

10 9 8 7 6 5 4

Typeset in Statendam, Brandon Grotesque,
Harman.
Printed in Turkey

Publisher's note
While every care has been taken in compiling
the recipes for this book, Watkins Media
Limited, or any other persons who have
been involved in working on this publication,
cannot accept responsibility for any errors
or omissions, inadvertent or not, that may
be found in the recipes or text, nor for
any problems that may arise as a result
of preparing one of these recipes. The
information in this book is not intended as a
substitute for professional medical advice and
treatment. If you are pregnant or are suffering
from any medical conditions or health
problems, it is recommended that you consult
a medical professional before following any
of the advice or practice suggested in this
book. Neither the author nor the publisher
can accept responsibility for any injuries
or damage incurred as a result of following
the information, exercises or therapeutic
techniques contained in this book.

Notes on the recipes
Unless otherwise stated:
Use medium fruit and vegetables.
Use medium (US large) organic or free-range
eggs. Use fresh herbs, spices and chillies.
Use granulated sugar. (Americans can use
ordinary granulated sugar when caster sugar
is specified.)
Do not mix metric, imperial and US cup
measurements:
1 tsp = 5ml 1 tbsp = 15ml 1 cup = 240ml

watkinspublishing.com

I dedicate this book to
all the magickians who've
supported me from day
one, to my brother who
has always known how
powerful I can be,
and to my beloved muggle
boyfriend Alex,
who believes in the magick
that is inside me.

CONTENTS

INTRODUCTION

It's understandable that when you think of the terms "witch" and "potion", the first thing that comes to mind is that iconic imagery of an old hag stirring her cauldron as wisps of steam rise from a mysterious liquid that bubbles and toils. This imagery has lingered on through generations, a testament to how powerful the archetype of the witch truly is. This archetype lives on and has evolved to meet today's technological and cultural advancements. Witches order spell correspondences off Amazon Prime (more on these later), shop for potion ingredients at the supermarket and sell their magickal wares on Etsy and Shopify, and at your local farmers' market. Every witch worth their salt knows how powerful the right potion can be. You might have picked this book up never having thought about potion-making before and are intrigued enough to give it a try. No matter if you're a seasoned witch, a baby witch just starting on their path or a curious purveyor of witchy cocktail concoctions, it might be time for you to tap into your own innate power and magick through the art of potion-making!

Potions are a cornerstone of witchcraft, yet many witches tend to avoid this kind of magick because it seems too complex or difficult in comparison to other spells or magickal workings. In reality, all of us are already expert potion makers and have been brewing potions most of our lives!

Have you ever made chicken soup for a sick friend, baked your bestie a birthday cake, cooked a romantic meal for a Tinder date or made yourself an extra-energizing cup of coffee in the morning? If you said yes to any of these then you already know the power of potions. The only difference between your grande pumpkin spice latte and an actual magickal potion is the intention that went into creating it.

The real magick behind potion-making is simple. You'll soon find within the pages of this book that imbuing your potion with the energy of magickal intention can transform a mundane cup of coffee or cocktail into a magickal brew!

So if you want to add potion-making to your magickal practice, dabble in crafty coffee-making or if you just want to mix a fun cocktail with your buddies this weekend, this is the book for you. Here's everything you need to know to get started with potions.

This book is filled to the brim with delicious potion drink recipes, half of which are non-alcoholic, with the remainder containing alcohol that can surely be omitted or substituted to your liking. Always remember that Intention > Ingredients in potion-making.

Share the magickal potions you've brewed online using #**PotionsBook**

MEET THE AUTHOR

STANDS UP

Hi! I'm Anaïs Alexandre, and I'm a witch.

the room yells in unison, "Hi Anaïs!"

For as long as I can remember I've always had a fascination with magic (a mundane term to denote fantasy in the media and sleight-of-hand stage magic) which slowly evolved into a fascination for real magick (the force that manifests change in your reality).

At first this meant I speed-read books like *Harry Potter* and *Lord of the Rings* and played fantasy games like

Dungeons & Dragons, *The Elder Scrolls* and The Witcher franchise. I think my love for all things fantasy led me to believe that mysteries were really outside the scope of possibility, only making themselves apparent as brief glimpses you could shrug off as coincidence. When I wasn't playing games I was sitting in the New Age aisle of Barnes & Noble with a stack of books up to my shoulder on subjects like astral projection, lucid dreaming, guardian angels, sigils, anything by Scott Cunningham, herbalism and tarot. For hours on end, day after day, I would be found sitting in my usual spot, straight up loitering and reading as much as I could before an employee would finally shoo me away or ask if I was ever going to buy something. The answer was always a polite, "No, I'm good thanks!" with a sly smile knowing I'd be in the same spot tomorrow.

Throughout the years I'd also had my fair share of otherworldly occurrences, from seeing a spirit in my kitchen, seeing glowing orbs float around the house, hearing voices of people who weren't there, knowing who was calling or at the door before any bell rang, and wishing things I really wanted into existence. Some of these occurrences were easier to dismiss than others, and while they did simultaneously frighten and intrigue me, what scared me more was bringing up these experiences to my religiously conservative and strict family. I taught myself how to self-soothe during those stressful moments and powered through them like the double Aries I am.

This passion for magick, though, began to slip out during casual conversations and even at a family dinner table. My conservative Catholic Haitian–American family had finally had enough of my 16-year-old goth-looking, magick-obsessed ass. They began to demonize my love of the magickal and blamed anything that went remotely wrong in my life on my affinity towards it. They would say all my troubles were a clear sign of punishment from the Catholic God. I began to internalize this "wrongness", and for a long time, I suppressed my desire to learn about anything related to the occult, having been worn down by the routine antagonization of my well-meaning family.

It wasn't until a few years later that I watched a YouTube video mentioning Psychokinesis, or PK, and parapsychology that I felt a familiar flicker of interest flutter somewhere inside me. This brought me back into the world of mysticism and the occult, but quickly I came to the realization that the PK community was a cold, methodical place I didn't resonate with. And so, I moved on to the next thing: Wicca.

Wicca was like a warm sunny hug that felt equally spiritual and right in my mind. It invited me into a worldwide community of others following the religious faith who all seemed to be varying degrees of sunshine, magick and rainbows. The tenet of "An it harm none, do what ye will" reassured me that I was in a safe space and that Wiccan ethics and values aligned closely with my Catholic roots, which quelled my Catholic guilt. I thought, "It's Witchcraft... but it's 'good' magick, so God probably won't smite me to the ground, right?"

One unforgettable moment happened days after I decided to pursue Wicca. I was home alone (as is common when most spooky things happen) and was writing in my Book of Shadows on my bed. That day I had been feeling really conflicted about my faith in Wicca and magick as a whole. I suddenly yelled aloud, "Ha! If magick is real, then the doorbell will ring right now!" and a second later the doorbell chimed loudly throughout the house. I jumped to my feet in shock, then reasoned that it was a coincidence. I decided to walk to the front door to see who it was. As I made my way to the front door I thought,

"Yeah, it's just eerie timing. It's probably just a delivery," but when I opened the door I didn't see a soul. Well, it took about 30 seconds flat for me to double-bolt lock the door and rush back to my room and back to work in my Book of Shadows.

As a baby Wiccan in my late teens all the way into my early twenties I finally felt at home. I followed the Wheel of the Year, celebrated the Sabbats and tended to my altar. Eventually I decided that maybe I could share my passion and knowledge with others on YouTube and Instagram. By the end of my first month posting about Wicca and magick online I had simultaneously reached my highest heights of joy as a content creator and lowest lows at seeing the hateful criticism and racism that flooded my comment section. It seemed that being a person of color as well as a Wiccan was not well received by the Wiccan community. At the same time the staunch religious masses hated me for the simple fact that I was a Witch and they continually quoted Bible verses at me. And so, wanting to protect myself and continue being a content creator, which had quickly become my life's North Star, I decided to rebrand myself as an Afro-Wiccan in the hopes that it'd make people feel more at ease and leave me alone. And it worked!

The experience of wanting to adapt my content to better suit my audience did not dissuade me from practicing Wicca. In fact, it pushed me to investigate other open practices and faiths and discover what else resonated with me. It was through this experience that I began incorporating rootwork (connecting with energy within objects, a basis for those practicing Hoodoo) into my practice. I'd transformed myself from a Wiccan into an Eclectic Witch. My practice still has ties to Wicca but has widened to include other elements of practices that best suit my needs.

I continued to churn out as much content as I could, hoping to answer deep-seated questions about magick and practicing Witchcraft through a mixture of anecdotal stories and practical advice. Over time I felt I was helping others realize that Witchcraft and magick weren't inherently evil in the slightest and actually helped make people smile and pursue their passions with vigor. Through the years as a content creator I grew to a place where I could be my authentic self within the Witchy community, fully accepted just as I am, without a label.

My relationship with the otherworldly continues to strengthen, and now I have the tools at my disposal to sense, read and work with a number of different energies. I've moved into a new magickal space in my life where I draw upon any number of open faiths and practices that interest me, creating an Eclectic Witchcraft all of my own.

WHAT ARE POTIONS AND HOW DO THEY WORK?

COMMON & STEREOTYPICAL VIEWS ON POTIONS

Some think it's absurd to believe that natural objects like herbs, crystals or waters mixed together into a potion can actually possess power. Herbalists throughout history, however, have always known that nature is powerful.

Take the bark of the white willow, for example: ancient herbalists have used it to relieve chronic pain, muscle aches and headaches for centuries, even before scientists "proved" its beneficial medicinal properties. Natural objects like herbs, flowers, crystals and waters contain real power and high vibrational energies that can be used for our benefit on both the physical and spiritual realms. All things in our natural world vibrate with energy at a particular frequency. The lower the frequency, the denser the energy of that object or person. Natural objects like crystals and herbs have a higher vibrational energy, and even being near them will in turn raise our own vibrational energy. The frequency at which any of us energetically vibrate will attract similar energy into our life.

I hope that through this book you'll begin learning and investigating just how powerful potions can be. The best – and, actually, the only – way to learn how powerful potions can be is by making them yourself or with a friend. They don't call witchcraft a practice for nothing!

Here are some potions basics and general tips you should know.

WHAT IS A POTION?

A potion is any mixture of ingredients that are imbued with energetic magickal intent and may have either magickal, healing or poisonous properties. (Although you won't find any poison in this book!)

Potions can be made with herbs, flowers, plants, roots, stems, essences, fruits, vegetables, crystals or other natural ingredients steeped in a base ingredient like water, alcohol or oil. If you decide to create your own potion, always remember to do your research to ensure that the herbs, oils, crystals and any other ingredients you're using are non-toxic and are safe to use.

Potions, like all forms of magick, work by following the Law of Sympathetic Magick and Correspondence, which explains that certain objects over time become associated with certain properties or attributes which allow them to act as a substitute for the latter. For example, roses have been associated as a symbol of love since Greek and Roman times, therefore in a magickal working related to love you can use roses as a correspondent. Correspondences are everyday objects said to be related to and which embody characteristics of more abstract conceptions or emotions. Using the Law of Sympathetic Magick and Correspondence, we will be incorporating potion ingredients into our spellwork to achieve the desired effect.

SOLID, LIQUID & GASEOUS POTIONS

Potions are created by mixing ingredients together to create a magickal mixture and can come in solid, liquid and gaseous states. Solid potions are items that have been mixed and then either placed over incense charcoal to smoke, or the mixture is cooked, frozen or baked into a solid. Liquid potions are what most people are familiar with and can be ingested (if they do not contain toxic ingredients) or can be applied to the skin as a wash, anointing oil or medicinal salve. These potions can also be used to asperge a space or person.

Gaseous potions are mixtures that are used to create sacred vapor, fumes, steam or smoke that a practitioner will use to suffumigate themselves or to cleanse objects or spaces through fumigation. Gaseous potions should always be researched with care to assure your own safety, as well as that of plant and animal friends around us.

This book will focus on supplying you with a list of liquid potions that are safe (and delicious!) to drink and that serve a magickal purpose!

Before we get started in creating our potions, it's important that we understand the terms commonly used by potion makers. Just imagine that Professor Snape is going to quiz you on these terms; it'll make them easier for you to remember!

Types of liquid potions include: asperges, baths, brews, cold oil infusions, decoctions, draughts, elixirs, herbal infusions, oil infusions, ointments, philtres, suspensions, tinctures, tonics and unguents.

ASPERGES

An asperges (or asperging) is a liquid magickal potion used in a ritual or rite to consecrate a group of people through the act of sprinkling the potion on their persons.

BATH

A liquid magickal potion that has been brewed with herbs and other ingredients and then added to a bathtub or large container filled with water for a person to bathe themselves in. One can also add a sachet to the water to imbue it with additional power and serve as aromatherapy.

BREW

A brew is the liquid form of a magickal potion.

COLD OIL INFUSIONS

A liquid potion in which herbs and other components are steeped in a carrier oil for an extended period at room temperature or cooler, in order to imbue that oil with the energetic powers of the components.

DECOCTION

A decoction is a liquid magickal potion in which bark, nuts, seeds and roots have been steeped in water.

DRAUGHT

A draught, pronounced "draft", is a liquid potion. "Draft" is often used in video games and fiction, like *The Elder Scrolls*, *Dungeons & Dragons* and *Harry Potter*.

ELIXIR

An elixir refers to a drinkable liquid magickal potion meant to give health and vitality. These are typically made by dissolving powders and extracts into a water and/or alcohol base and then are sweetened with honey, syrup, mashed fruits or other sweeteners.

HERBAL INFUSION

An herbal infusion is made by adding herbs to a base of water, pure ethyl alcohol, fruit or vegetable juice, milk, oil, butter or honey. These can be added to other concoctions, such as baths and washes, or they can be used to anoint a person or object and are a great alternative to anointing oils for those with skin sensitivities.

OIL INFUSION

This is a magickal potion where essential oils that have been extracted from plants are mixed with other fragrance oils, cosmetic oils or a base oil (almond oil, olive oil, vegetable oil, jojoba oil or grapeseed oil).

OINTMENT

An ointment is made by infusing a fat-based lotion or beeswax-based balm with enchanted herbs and other ingredients. One of the most famous types of witch ointment is the flying ointment, with folklore stating that witches used it to fly on their brooms during Sabbath. Flying ointments are now believed to have had hallucinogenic properties that induced trance states and astral projection. Please do not make flying ointments, as they can be dangerous.

PHILTRE

A philtre is a drinkable love potion intended to make the drinker fall in love with the person who created it. For those that have played the video game *The Witcher*, Petri's Philtre may come to mind, but this philtre had the different effect of enhancing the Witcher abilities.

SUSPENSION

A suspension is a drinkable liquid magickal potion with medicinal properties similar to an elixir, in which the particles of the components can't fully dissolve and is intended to be shaken before drinking.

TINCTURE

A tincture is a liquid magickal potion in which herbs have infused 80–140-proof ethyl alcohol (80-proof vodka). Examples of mundane tinctures would be flavoring extracts like vanilla extract or almond extract. High-proof limoncello could also be considered a tincture.

TONIC

A tonic is a drinkable liquid magickal potion in which herbs have infused any water-based mixture to serve a magickal purpose.

UNGUENT

An unguent is a liquid magickal potion used as an anointing oil that is safe to use on a person or an object.

THE BASICS OF MAKING A POTION

CONTAINERS AND VESSELS

Understanding what container you'll be brewing your potion in as well as what type of container you'll be storing your potion in are just as important as the ingredients you use to make it!

Typically, practitioners avoid the use of metal cooking pots, as certain ingredients can react with metal, most notably any type of citrus. It's also believed that metal can change the energetic vibration of certain ingredients, which could change the effect or properties of the potion you are creating.

The use of metal cooking pots being used for potion-making is a highly debated topic, as are most topics in witchcraft. There are some that believe using certain types of metal cooking pots actually add amazing earth magick to the potion. The ultimate decision of whether to use a metal pot lies with you as an individual and what you feel comfortable with. Suggested alternatives to using a metal pot are glass, ceramic, clay or stone cookware.

KITCHEN WITCH TOOLS (ONLY FOR MAGICKAL USE, NOT EVERYDAY USE)

Mortar and Pestle: to grind ingredients, in order to release oils and activate herbs

Dry electric coffee grinder: should only be used to grind dry, finely crushed or chopped potion ingredients

Ritual knife or athame

Censer or incense burner (or any bowl half-filled with sand)

Candles of varying lengths and colors

Ceramic or glass bowls for mixing and steeping; glass containers work exceptionally well when imbuing potions with solar/lunar light energy

Eye droppers to infuse brews with oils and other liquid substances

Sieve/fine mesh strainer, coffee filter or muslin cheesecloth to strain solid material from liquid potion

Glass bottles with cork stoppers/lids to store your completed potions

Journal to record how you customized potions to your liking

CLEANSING YOUR TOOLS AND SPACE

After you've physically washed and cleansed the tools you'll be using to make your potions, you'll also want to energetically cleanse them. Giving your entire ritual space or kitchen a good energetic cleanse is a great idea too! I give some ideas on how to cleanse your space on p. 62.

BASIC INGREDIENTS

CORRESPONDENCES

What type of ingredients will you be incorporating into your potion?

Each type of plant, herb, crystal or other correspondence you incorporate in your potion possesses a distinct power in and of itself. By harmoniously combining the right ingredients we create a vibrationally synchronous force that will attract our goal.

BASE LIQUID

You might remember from chemistry class that you always need a solvent. Typically, the liquid used in potion-making is the universal solvent: water. Other solvents can and will be used in the recipes within this book. If water is being used as the base solvent, the energetic level of the water should be taken into consideration.

WATER

Spring waters or rainwater are considered to be living waters, or waters that retain high energetic vibrations.

Distilled water or tap water are commonly believed to be inert forms of water, having been entrapped in water systems or plastic containers for an indefinite amount of time.

Mineral waters or sea waters contain salts and other minerals that are not typically used in potion-making because consuming foods or liquids with high salinity levels does present health risks. Additionally, due to the high mineral content in these waters, they may react with other correspondences and ingredients within the potion.

Crystal-infused waters are another form of energetically viable water. Crystals can be used to raise the energy of inert waters by placing one in it. Some crystals can dissolve or leech toxic material in the liquids they're submerged in, making that liquid poisonous to consume. The best and most safe crystals to use for potion-making are the quartz family (particularly the clearer forms): clear quartz, citrine, amethyst and rose quartz. If you decide to use a safe non-toxic crystal in your potion, make sure it is sanitized before you submerge in room temperature or cooled liquids. If you're still concerned about adding the crystal directly into the liquid, you can put it inside a small mason jar and then place this jar in the larger container holding your potion.

Caution: Do not submerge a crystal into a potion if you are not absolutely certain that it is safe to do so. If in any doubt, please put inside a mason jar to ensure the crystal does not come into direct contact with the liquid.

Sparkling or carbonated waters are a great way to add effervescence and whimsy to a liquid potion. Just be mindful: if it's sparkling mineral water, the minerals can sometimes react poorly with other ingredients.

No matter what type of water you're using, make sure it's clean and filtered prior to use.

FRUIT AND VEGETABLE JUICE

Organic and naturally sourced vegetables and fruits that have been juiced at home are best, but not everyone has the time or resources for this, so use whatever you have available to you! Juices are great because they can imbue color magick into potions. Each fruit, vegetable, herb, leaf, stem or root contains unique properties that are distinct to them.

ALCOHOL

The use of alcohol in the recipes of this book is purely optional. If you do choose to incorporate alcohol in the recipes, here is a short list of the ones used based on the correspondences they're made from:

Absinthe: an anise-flavored spirit derived from botanicals. Its correspondences are independence, psychic enhancement, love, passion, happiness, protection, purification, youth, luck, nightmare prevention, vitality, virility and curse-breaking.

Beer: brewed from cereal grains like malted barley, wheat, corn or rice. Its correspondences are love, healing, protection, prosperity, fertility, marriage, financial luck, growth, transformation, healing and sleep.

Cider: made from the fermented juice of apples. Its correspondences are immortality, health and love.

Gin: derived from redistilling ethanol in the presence of juniper berries and other botanicals. Its correspondences are health and protection.

Liqueurs: are distilled spirits sweetened and spiced by fruit, cream, herbs, spices, flowers or nuts. Their correspondences are connection, prosperity and love.

Rum: made from molasses, honey or sugarcane juice. Its correspondences are clarity, love and strength.

Vodka: made through distilling cereal grains or potatoes. Its correspondences are stability, truth and vitality.

Whiskey: distilled from fermented grains like barley, corn, rye and wheat. Its correspondences are protection, strength, love, healing, fertility, marriage, financial luck, prosperity, growth and transformation.

NON-ALCOHOLIC LIQUID BASES USED IN POTIONS:

COFFEE

The closer you can get to freshly ground roasted coffee the better, but using instant coffee grinds will work in a pinch! Its correspondence is vitality, joy, happiness, diligence and energy.

TEA

Many potions can be made simply by submerging tea bags that have been selected based on the components within the sachet. Tea bags really are a potion maker's life hack. The correspondence of the tea bag is directly related to the herbs included in each mix.

MILK

Dairy milks are associated with fertility, love, health and protection.

Non-dairy milks

Almond: healing, prosperity, wisdom, overcoming addiction, abundance, luck.

Cashew: prosperity, increased energy, communication.

Coconut: allure, confidence, diversity, flexibility, protection, peace, meditation, removal of negative influences, love, binding, psychic visions.

Flax: beauty, healing, protection, money, psychic enhancement.

Hazelnut: fertility, luck, mental enhancement, wisdom, dreams, divination, spirit work, wishes.

Hemp: positive energy, manifestation, healing, protection, peace, mediation, removal of negative influences, love, binding, psychic visions.

Macadamia: prosperity.

Oat: grounding, prosperity, beauty, healing, health.

Pea: love and prosperity.

Pistachio: breaking curses, hexes or trances, grounding and divination.

Rice: fertility, abundance, blessings, protection, rain, security, wealth.

Sunflower: protection, success, positive energy, confidence, happiness.

Soy: is associated with protection, psychic awareness, spirituality.

OTHER LIQUIDS USED IN POTIONS

Kombucha: is made from sweetened teas with a live bacterial or yeast culture to ferment it.

Oils: magickal correspondences dependent on the source of the oil.

Rose water and rose extract: rose promotes love and happiness. You will find recipes that use rose water and rose extract in this book. Please note the difference: rose extract is much more intense in flavor, and no more than 1 tsp should be used per serving.

Sweeteners: in general all sweeteners are associated with love, compassion, steadfastness. When I mention using a "sweetener of your choice", this could include honey, agave, maple syrup, molasses, stevia, caster or white sugar, coconut sugar or date sugar.

HARVESTING PLANTS AND HERBS

Ideal places to harvest mature plants would be from a trusted garden or farm where they have been grown organically without the use of pesticides or chemicals. It is best to avoid harvesting plants near polluted or stagnant water sources or near busy streets or roadways.

The way you harvest your ingredients is important to consider as well. When we harvest herbs we are essentially asking the plant to ally with us on a singular goal. We should always approach these requests with respect and offer a gift, usually fresh water poured at the plants base as a gesture of appreciation for agreeing to help us. When harvesting plants or other natural ingredients, you should be mindful to avoid over-harvesting and assure the plant will continue to thrive.

CLOCKWISE OR COUNTERCLOCKWISE

Stirring your potion clockwise (deosil) draws in attractive forces and positive vibrations to bless or consecrate.

Stirring your potion counter-clockwise (widdershins) deflects or dispels energies to rid yourself of negative aspects from your life.

VEGAN SUBSTITUTES

Egg white: substitute with aquafaba.

Egg yolk: substitute with creamy plant/nut milk.

Condensed milk: substitute with creamy plant/nut milk + sweet syrup like agave.

Half and half, heavy whipping cream, whipped cream: substitute with coconut cream.

Honey: substitute with agave syrup or simple syrup.

WITCHCRAFT BASICS

Witchcraft is a practice, not a religion. While a religion has faith-based followers who hold to a distinct set of ethics, values and moral code, witchcraft does not. Witchcraft is a practice in which a practitioner manipulates energy to bring about the change they'd like to see in their reality. Witchcraft has no universal laws or ethical codes to abide by and is not a faith. So yes, you can be a follower of a certain religious faith and also practice Witchcraft. Whether you feel it's appropriate or not is up to you.

Within this tome you'll find pages brimming with magickal potions. It's important to note that the main distinction between simply mixing ingredients together to make a drink and creating a magickal potion is the act of intention. When you intend for a result to happen through each step of the potion-making process, then – and only then – are you creating magick. And who doesn't need a little more magick in their life?

The included potions are not intended to be manipulative in nature, and it is my sincere hope that good-natured folks looking for a fun magickal time are the ones happily browsing through these pages. Always remember that power comes from intention, which is the magickal ingredient for every potion listed here. If your ingredient is soured by cruelty, then that is what you'll consume, so be mindful and be sweet, my dear.

To cover some witchcraft basics, I've included a few terms you'll want to be familiar with in order to gain a better understanding while using this book.

Magick: an energetic force that brings about change in our reality.

Witch: a practitioner of magick skilled at shaping their reality to align with their desires.

Spell: a magickal working with a clear and focused intention.

Potion: a magickal mixture, either solid, liquid or gaseous, created to manifest a goal or desire, and made while focusing on an intention.

Incantation: the words, song, poem or phraseology used in a working.

Enchantment: the act of energetically empowering a person or object.

Correspondence: the ability of a person, place or thing to carry magickal associations due to its similarity or connection with a magickal concept, energy, trait or characteristic.

Invoke: to willingly surrender your autonomy to a deity or outside energy in order to draw power from that source.

Evoke: the act of requesting energetic assistance or guidance in a magickal working or petition.

Energy: the life force that vibrates within all living things in our universe and has the ability to be manipulated to aggregate in a desire.

Imbue: the act of willing energy to transfer and aggregate in another object or person.

WHAT IS MAGICK?

Magick is a force that allows one to bring about changes in their reality through manifestation.

This definition might seem vague and that's because it is so tricky to define. I liken it to defining love. We can say that love is both a biochemical evolutionary con job as well as deep emotion and psychological resonance toward a person, place or thing.

Magick, in my opinion, works in a similar way. We as practitioners apply the force of attention, focus and will to bring about change in our lives, and also ally ourselves with energies and natural correspondences like plants and herbs through spells and rituals to help us reach that same goal. Often, the most successful magick is done by combining magickal and mundane acts to get closer to achieving your goal. For example, when creating a money-drawing potion, you'd get the best results if you coupled the act of creating that potion along with mundane acts of applying for jobs that pay more, cutting down on your spending or creating a savings account. Being a magickal practitioner means putting your faith not only in the realm of science but also in our own inherent power to bring about the changes we'd like to see in our lives.

The process by which magick works is like the snowball effect. Imagine that your desire is to create a snowball larger than life. There are two ways to achieve that desire. You can either expend physical energy by rolling a small snowball into a larger one over a long period of time, or you can create a small snowball and climb a hill, then roll your snowball down the side of the hill, allowing it to amass more snow more quickly than you ever could by any other means. This is the power of magickal intention. The climb up the mountain (mundane work) coupled with your clear intent to see the snowball grow (at the precipice of the hill) allows the change in the snowball to manifest, and magick brings about the change you want to see (a large snowball at the bottom of the hill). Magick is your ace in the hole, your secret advantage, and it is a key resource you may want to start tapping into more often.

One of the greatest misconceptions of those getting started in practicing magick is understanding how it fundamentally works with respect to time. Many hope for and wish the effects will happen instantaneously. While magick can expedite results for us, it does not happen at the snap of a finger. In our natural world, there is no living thing that does not have a growth period or show growth over time. Following with this natural law we need to apply patience and understanding of how our world operates, to recognize that effects or results of a magickal working will follow this same natural pattern and present results or growth toward a goal over time, not instantaneously.

Another topic that is not widely discussed is what magick really is. At the core of any magickal working is energy. Energy and magick are interchangeable. It is energy being raised and focused through a desire or intention that creates the changes we desire. So if we look at a magickal working at its core, you will find that it's made up of the focus and will of an individual. You do not need any other attributes, ingredients, tools, conceptions or materials to manifest change in your life through magickal means. The only thing that's mandatory is you and your willpower to focus on your intention and create change in your life.

Intention is key. Someone putting these ingredients together for a potion recipe in this book for fun and giggles will thoroughly enjoy how tasty each potion is and how fun it is to create them. If that same person had strong intent behind creating these potions, they might be surprised by the wonderful things that start coming their way!

HOW TO USE THE RECIPES

ICONS

Each recipe has three icons to help you decide which potion to make, whatever your mood or time you have available.

DIFFICULTY

Starred icons show how challenging the potion is to make. One star is easy, two is medium, three is a little more difficult.

ALCOHOLIC OR ALCOHOL-FREE

These icons tell you whether the potion is intended to contain alcohol or not. But remember, some of the recipes with an alcohol icon come with a variation to make them alcohol-free.

SEASON

A flower for spring, a sun for summer, a leaf for autumn and a snowflake for winter; whatever the weather, this will help you to keep your potions seasonal, fresh and aligned with the wheel of the year.

All recipes serve one witch, unless otherwise stated.

DISCOVER ANAÏS'S ONLINE CAFÉ

I show how to create, pour and garnish each potion in this book on my tiktok channel (@potionsbook). Simply scan this QR code to visit!

LOVE

POTIONS

LOVE POTIONS

There are no recipes in this book that would attempt to control or manipulate anyone against their will. Instead, the potions laid before you are intended to enhance your magnetism for loving energies.

There is nothing more powerful than love. It has the power to transform whatever it touches into the greatest form of itself. Interest becomes passion, kindness becomes altruism, and friendliness becomes adoration. Love is what we're all seeking, whether we want to admit it or not. We are constantly in search of love from others through acceptance, empathy and understanding. We can also deny ourselves self-love every time we indulge in negative self-talk. If only we could see just how lovable we already are, just as we are, each and every one of us, the world would be a less cringe-worthy place to live.

Love spells and potions are the most common request the witchy community receives, and I can attest to that. With these requests comes a deep sense of loneliness, envy or need to feel wanted. We've all likely experienced these feelings of emptiness at one point or another and I want to tell you that the easiest way to fill that void is through the act of SELF-LOVE.

That may not be the answer you were looking for, but it's the one I'm giving you because it's true. When I got dumped by my ex a few years back and I felt like hot garbage, undeserving of love and affection, one critical decision made all the difference in the world to me. What finally brought me to my feet was investing time and energy into activities, clubs and projects that I was passionate about. When you do things that make you happy and you spend the majority of your time doing what you love, it shows inside and out. You shine like a diamond and draw other happy people toward you like a magnet. When you're happy the world can't help but be dazzled by you. This, my friends, is the only love magick you'll ever need.

But I understand there will be a few folks who just want that cute person in class to notice them, or a co-worker to take them out for drinks. And while it is not possible to evoke genuine feelings of love within another person, you can bring on feelings associated with love. Here's some recipes that aid in doing just that.

For vegan substitutes please see page 28.

CORRESPONDENCES

INCENSE

benzoin, dragon's blood, honeysuckle, rose-scented incense

CRYSTALS TO WORK WITH FOR LOVE SPELLS

amber, beryl, calcite, chrysocolla, emerald, jade, lapis lazuli, lepidolite, moonstone, pearl, pink tourmaline, rose quartz, sapphire, topaz, turquoise

DAY OF THE WEEK FOR LOVE SPELLS

Friday

PLANET FOR LOVE SPELLS

Venus

ZODIAC SIGNS FOR LOVE SPELLS

Libra, Cancer

MOON PHASES FOR LOVE SPELLS

Full Moon, Dark Moon

BURNIN' LOVE

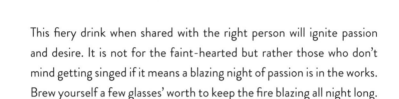

This fiery drink when shared with the right person will ignite passion and desire. It is not for the faint-hearted but rather those who don't mind getting singed if it means a blazing night of passion is in the works. Brew yourself a few glasses' worth to keep the fire blazing all night long.

Key correspondences included in this drink are:

VANILLA. The subtle seductress that has been used throughout history as an aphrodisiac. Vanilla can also be used in workings to soothe, to calm, for personal empowerment and good luck.

RED CHILLI. Red chillies have a long history of use in "hot footing" works of magick to banish people from your life but is also commonly used as a way to spice up any romantic relationship.

CHERRIES. A wonderful fruit to add to workings of love. Cherries have been used for attracting and stimulating love for centuries.

CINNAMON SUGAR. One of the most excellent combinations for love magick; it both heats up love situations and also sweetens the desired target towards you. Mix 100g/3½oz/½ cup caster/granulated sugar with 2 tbsp ground cinnamon to use in your potions.

ROSEMARY. This herb was worn by medieval brides and also carried by wedding guests as a token of love and virtue. When included in potions or spells it will encourage faithfulness in your lover.

INGREDIENTS

★ Pinch of dried chilli/hot pepper flakes

★ 3 tbsp cinnamon sugar (see opposite)

★ 1 tsp vanilla extract

★ 2 tbsp grenadine syrup

★ Ice cubes

★ 125ml/4fl oz/ ½ cup cherry cola

★ 60ml/2fl oz/ ¼ cup Fireball whiskey (optional)

Magickal Garnish
★ Fresh rosemary sprig (singed)

RITUAL

HOLD THE IMAGE OF THE PERSON IN YOUR MIND AS YOU CREATE THIS POTION. IMAGINE ALL THE LOVING & HEATED SCENARIOS YOU'D LIKE TO EXPERIENCE WITH THEM. DON'T GET TOO ABSORBED IN THE FANTASY OR YOU'LL NEVER FINISH MAKING THE POTION!

METHOD

★ In a small bowl, stir together the chilli/hot pepper flakes with the cinnamon sugar.

★ Wet the rim of your serving glass with water, then dip it into the spicy cinnamon sugar.

★ Keeping the object of your attraction fixed in your mind, add the rest of the ingredients to the glass, adding the cherry cola last.

★ Finally, garnish with a small sprig of rosemary that's been gently singed using a lighter or flame. The goal is not to burn the entire sprig to a crisp but rather to burn it for only a second to release its oils.

LOVE ORACLE

If you've ever wistfully pulled a flower from the ground and whispered, "they love me, they love me not" while plucking out each petal, then this drink is for you. That simple act is really one of divination, specifically floromancy. This dreamy green drink (green's also the color of the heart chakra) will let you play out your fairytale dreams and give you a glimpse into the future of your love life. Simply trade plucking petals for chewing boba balls to discover what love lies in your future.

Key correspondences included in this drink are:

JASMINE. Jasmine is often used in love-drawing magick and is said to attract spiritually pure love (as opposed to spicy flings).

GINGER. Typically used in workings of love, protection, magickal powers and healing. It's also often used to ignite passion and love due to its spicy nature.

SWEET BASIL. Invites the concept of a loving relationship into your life and aids in bringing real love and good luck closer to you.

ABSINTHE. An anise-flavored spirit derived from botanicals like wormwood, anise and fennel. Each of these botanicals are associated with drawing love and happiness into your life. The wormwood within absinthe stimulates and enhances psychic abilities.

INGREDIENTS

- ★ 3 tbsp tapioca pearls/boba balls
- ★ 2 tbsp caster/granulated sugar
- ★ 125ml/4fl oz/½ cup boiling water
- ★ 1 jasmine white tea bag
- ★ 3 sweet basil leaves
- ★ 2.5cm/1in piece of fresh root ginger, grated
- ★ 1 tbsp absinthe (optional)

Magickal Garnish

- ★ ½ tsp jasmine buds
- ★ 2 sweet basil leaves
- ★ Crystallized ginger

RITUAL

COUNT THROUGH EACH BOBA BALL YOU CHEW – THE FIRST BOBA BALL DECIDING WHETHER "THEY LOVE YOU" AND THE SECOND DECIDING "THEY LOVE YOU NOT". CONTINUE CHEWING EACH BOBA INDIVIDUALLY UNTIL YOU FINISH THE BREW, TO DETERMINE THE TRUE ANSWER.

METHOD

★ Cook your tapioca pearls/boba balls according to the packet instructions. Once prepared, stir in the sugar until dissolved and set aside to cool.

★ In a ceramic or glass mug, create an herbal infusion by pouring the boiling water over the tea bag, then add in the 3 basil leaves and the fresh ginger. Set aside to cool.

★ Once the herbal infusion has cooled, strain the liquid through a sieve/fine mesh strainer and discard the solid material.

★ Place your tapioca pearls/boba balls in a serving glass, then pour in the infusion.

★ Add the absinthe, if using, and stir the drink to mix evenly.

★ Garnish with jasmine buds, basil leaves and crystallized ginger to represent the budding romance of you and your future significant other.

SWEET ON ME

It's time you had a taste of the sweet life (I'm using all my strength not to finish that with "Zack and Cody"). If you're looking to become the candy apple of someone's eye, or you desire preferential treatment from everyone that crosses your path, you should give this drink a try. That eye candy you've been ogling will return the favor, lickety-split.

Key correspondences included in this drink are:

HONEY. Like other sweeteners, honey has long been associated with a deep, resonating connection, enduring love and prosperity. There's a reason the sweetest part of a relationship is called the honeymoon.

LAVENDER. Associated with beauty and love.

JASMINE. Jasmine is used in love-drawing magick and is said to attract spiritually pure love (as opposed to spicy flings).

APPLE. Apple is known as the fruit of love. To make candy apple slices, in a saucepan over a medium heat, mix 240ml/8fl oz/1 cup water with 400g/14oz/2 cups caster/granulated sugar. Bring to the boil for 8 mins without stirring. Take off the heat, dip fresh apple slices into the syrup and cool on a wire/cooling rack.

RUM. Rum is made from molasses, honey or sugarcane juice and as such works wonderfully in love magick to bring a sweet romance.

INGREDIENTS

- ★ 60ml/2fl oz/ ¼ cup boiling water
- ★ 1 tsp jasmine buds
- ★ ¼ tsp lavender buds
- ★ 1 tbsp honey, plus extra for drizzling
- ★ 60ml/2fl oz/ ¼ cup apple juice
- ★ 60ml/2fl oz/ ¼ cup passion fruit juice
- ★ 60ml/2fl oz/ ¼ cup rum (optional)
- ★ Scoop of vanilla ice cream
- ★ Ice cubes

Magickal Garnish
- ★ Candy apple slices (see opposite)

RITUAL

IT'S TIME TO TURN YOUR BLENDER INTO A MAGICKAL TOOL. AS THE POTION BLENDS, REPEAT THE FOLLOWING INCANTATION: "AS THE LOVELY FRUITS OF THIS POTION SPIN RAPIDLY, SO TOO SHALL YOUR LOVE REVOLVE AROUND ME."

METHOD

★ In a ceramic or glass mug, create an herbal infusion by pouring the boiling water over the jasmine and lavender buds. Stir in the honey and allow to steep for 5 mins.

★ Once the herbal infusion has cooled, strain the liquid through a sieve/fine mesh strainer and discard the solid material.

★ Put the herbal infusion and other ingredients in a blender. Pulse to distribute the ice evenly, then blend for 30 secs.

★ Pour the potion into a tall glass and drizzle the shape of two intertwined hearts with honey on top.

★ Garnish the rim of the glass with candy apple slices.

ROSE-COLORED GLASSES

Whether you'd like to swap your justified cynical worldview for a cheerier set of rose-tinted glasses, or if you'd just like someone you got off on the wrong foot with to see you in a better light, this drink is sure to brighten up your day!

Key correspondences included in this drink are:

PRIMROSE. Primrose is a flower that's deeply connected to the moon and the feminine aspect within each of us. It helps in communication and building strong relationships with our loved ones. Dried primrose buds and petals can easily be found online.

STRAWBERRY. Strawberry helps in all matters of love by overcoming barriers and issues in your way. Strawberries are also associated with good luck, fertility and providing dedication to solve problems and bring about a happy resolution.

ROSE QUARTZ. A phenomenal crystal of universal love. It works wonders for all matters of the heart and assists in workings to encourage unconditional love, self-love, romantic love, friendship, platonic love and every facet of love itself. It's a crystal that is safe to submerge directly into water, but caution should be used if it's a fragmented stone with crystal sediment falling off.

INGREDIENTS

★ 125ml/4fl oz/
½ cup rose water

★ 175g/6oz/1¾ cup
strawberries

★ 50g/1¾oz/
¼ cup caster/
granulated sugar

★ Ice cubes

★ 150ml/5fl oz/
scant ⅔ cup
light-colored
soda

Magickal Garnish

★ Sugared rose/
primrose petals
(To make:
lightly coat
petals in an egg
white wash,
then dip them
into caster/
granulated
sugar and leave
to dry for a
few hours.)

METHOD

★ In a ceramic or glass mug, create an herbal crystal infusion by submerging the crystal directly (or indirectly using a mason jar) in the cool rose water and allowing it to infuse for 3 mins. Please ensure the crystal has been physically cleansed in water first.

★ In the meantime, blend the strawberries and sugar in a blender until smooth.

★ Transfer the strawberry purée to a glass or ceramic cooking pot and cook on a low heat for 6 mins, reducing the mixture to a syrup consistency. Set aside to cool.

★ Strain the rose quartz infusion through a sieve/fine mesh strainer. Set the quartz on a counter nearby while you assemble the drink.

★ In a glass filled with ice, add your strawberry syrup. Then add your quartz infusion and finally top the drink off with the light-colored soda. Garnish with sugared petals.

RITUAL

HOLD A ROSE QUARTZ BETWEEN BOTH HANDS, IN A PRAYER POSITION. STAND FACING WEST. CLOSE YOUR EYES AND ASK THE ELEMENT OF WATER TO WASH AWAY PAST PERCEPTIONS. GIVE A SMALL BOW OF THANKS AND THEN BEGIN CREATING THE POTION.

#ILOVEME

Self-love gets a bad rap nowadays; many are jaded by online gurus slinging self-love advice left and right. This is because we, as a society, value the opinions others have of us more than our own. Combined with negative self-talk, and comparing ourselves to others, you get a generation of humans who believe loving themselves is an unattainable goal only self-enlightened influencers can achieve.

The easiest first step on the road to liking yourself is to be a better friend to yourself. The next time you indulge in judging your actions, your appearance or achievements, respond to that negative self-talk like a loving best friend or parent would. If what you're telling yourself isn't something a loving person in your life would say, replace it with what a loving person would say. Give yourself a dose of self-love today!

Key correspondences included in this drink are:

CARDAMOM. A spice that has been used in love magick for centuries due to its association with stimulating warmth between people and encouraging love within a person.

CINNAMON. Associated with feelings of coziness, strength, empowerment and safety. It's also widely used in workings for healing.

NUTMEG. Known to bring good luck, prosperity and financial success to your endeavors.

INGREDIENTS

* ★ 1 egg yolk
* ★ 1 tbsp condensed milk
* ★ 3 tbsp double/ heavy cream
* ★ 125ml/4fl oz/ ½ cup boiling water
* ★ 2 cardamom tea bags

* ★ Pinch of ground cinnamon
* ★ Pinch of ground nutmeg

Magickal Garnish

* ★ Marshmallows, cut into heart shapes

RITUAL

EACH TIME YOU TAKE A SIP OF THE DRINK, REPEAT THE WORDS "I LOVE ME" TO YOURSELF, EITHER ALOUD OR IN YOUR HEAD, UNTIL YOU FINISH THE DRINK.

METHOD

★ In a ceramic or glass bowl, over a pot of steaming water, whisk together the egg yolk, condensed milk and cream until a light yellow custard has formed.

★ In a ceramic or glass mug, create an herbal infusion by pouring the boiling water over the cardamom tea bags and allowing it to steep for 3 mins. Discard the tea bags.

★ Top with the custard mixture and a sprinkling of ground cinnamon and nutmeg.

★ Garnish with heart-shaped marshmallows.

cleansing

CLEANSING

POTIONS

CLEANSING POTIONS

Cleansing rituals are in every witch's toolbelt. We routinely perform physical and energetic cleansings on our magickal tools, items, spaces, ourselves and our environment. It allows us to essentially return things to their default setting, energetically speaking. Once we've performed cleansing rituals we follow up with protection rituals. Cleansing and protection are the perfect magickal pairing, like salt and pepper.

There are many reasons to energetically cleanse. You might have recently experienced a breakup and want to cleanse the space of lingering feelings in order to move on. Or you might have moved into a new dorm, apartment or home and want to start things off with a clean slate. Whatever the reason, there are many options available to you.

Typical ways to cleanse a space are through using sacred smoke, sound, light, incantations, blessed salted waters or perhaps calling in energetic allies to assist in the rites. Utilizing the power of the elements is another way to cleanse objects. You can do this in the following way:

Earth: Bury an item with salt or within the earth to allow the energies to disperse and be absorbed by the soil.

Water: Hold the item under running water, ensuring prior to doing that the item is not water-soluble or can be water-damaged.

Fire: Passing non-flammable ritual tools over the flame of a candle or small fire is a method of cleansing. Smoke-cleansing is another popular method of purifying objects, people and spaces.

Air: Smoke-cleansing using herbs associated with purification is a great way to practice cleansing. (Note: white sage and palo santo are currently over-harvested so it's advised to seek out alternatives like lavender, cedar or sweetgrass. White sage is also sacred to many indigenous people and is an intrinsic part of a sacred practice called smudging. Neither the act nor the word should be used by non-indigenous people.)

For vegan substitutes please see page 28.

CORRESPONDENCES

INCENSE

bay, eucalyptus, frankincense, mugwort, myrrh, lavender, pine, rose geranium, rosemary, sandalwood, St John's wort, valerian, vervain

CRYSTALS TO WORK FOR CLEANSING SPELLS

amber, clear quartz, chrysocolla, diamond, fluorite, garnet, peridot, selenite, smoky quartz

DAY OF THE WEEK FOR CLEANSING SPELLS

Saturday

PLANET FOR CLEANSING SPELLS

Saturn

ZODIAC SIGN FOR CLEANSING SPELLS

Capricorn

MOON PHASE FOR CLEANSING SPELLS

Waning Moon

PURIFIED

This purifying tonic is filled with cleansing properties that will clear away stagnant and troublesome energies around you – in your physical space or on an emotional level. Using the power of citrusy yuzu and turmeric, you'll be able to soothe any inflamed situation and emotional pain you may be experiencing with a single gulp.

Key correspondences included in this drink are:

TURMERIC. Turmeric is used in magickal workings involving banishment, protection, cleansing, clarifying, removing negative energies, vitality, strength and healing.

GIN. Gin is derived from redistilling ethanol in the presence of juniper berries and other botanicals. As such, gin is associated with health, healing and protection.

GINGER. Ginger is typically used in workings of love, protection, magickal powers and healing. It's also often used to ignite passion and love due to its spicy nature.

YUZU. An Asian hybrid citrus fruit traditionally thought to ward off illness and promote well-being. It is refreshing and uplifting, while calming to the mind.

INGREDIENTS

★ 3½ tbsp water

★ 2 tbsp yuzu juice (or freshly squeezed lime juice)

★ ¼ tsp ground turmeric

★ ¼ tsp ground ginger

★ 3 sprigs fresh mint

★ 2 tbsp sweetener of your choice

★ 2 tbsp gin

Magickal Garnish

★ Yuzu slices (or lime slices)

RITUAL

AS YOU DRINK THIS POTION, IMAGINE IT FILLING YOUR BEING WITH BRIGHT YELLOW LIGHT WHICH BURNS AWAY ANY TOXIC ENERGIES WITHIN AND AROUND YOU.

METHOD

★ In a small saucepan, mix the water, yuzu juice, ground turmeric, ground ginger, 2 sprigs of mint and the sweetener.

★ Bring to a simmer for about 3 mins, then turn off the heat. Allow to cool slightly.

★ Stir in the gin and remaining mint.

★ Pour into a heatproof serving glass, garnish with yuzu slices and enjoy.

RESTORE

This potion is perfect when you've had a long day but still need a bit more staying power to accomplish those last-minute tasks. Ally with the power of taro to connect you with the grounding and cleansing energy of Mother Earth. With taro by your side, you'll be able to tackle incoming challenges with ease and say ta-ta to your worries.

Key correspondence included in this drink:

TARO. Ube or taro is a purple sweet potato that is linked to enchanting a friendly relationship, increasing harmony, grounding yourself, proving a nourishing and nurturing connection to the earth as well as ancestors that have passed on, and, finally, inspiring love and sensuality.

INGREDIENTS

★ 2 tbsp tapioca pearls/boba balls (optional)

★ 1 black tea bag

★ 125ml/4fl oz/ ½ cup boiling water

★ 1 tbsp taro powder

★ 2 tbsp sweetener of your choice

★ 125ml/4fl oz/ ½ cup whole milk/half and half

RITUAL

PRIOR TO DRINKING THIS POTION, EMBRACE YOURSELF (YES, I MEAN GIVE YOURSELF AN AFFECTIONATE HUG!) AND SAY ALOUD: "MY ROOTS GROW STRONGER BY THE DAY, ANCIENT POWER WITHIN ME STAY."

METHOD

★ If using tapioca pearls/boba balls, prepare according to the packet instructions. Set aside to cool.

★ Steep the tea bag in the boiling water for 3 mins, then allow to cool.

★ In a bowl, whisk the cooled black tea with the taro powder until well combined, then whisk in the sweetener until dissolved.

★ In a tall serving glass, first add the prepared tapioca pearls, if using, then add the tea and taro mixture and finally top with the milk/half and half. Stir and enjoy!

CLARITY

★ 🍸 ☀

The elderberry is a legendary fruit that's not only tart and sweet but has been nicknamed "the whole medicine chest". This medicinal berry is ideal for those seeking the ultimate cleanse from toxins in the body. This elderberry elixir will heal what ails you on a physical, emotional and spiritual level. Just what the witch doctor ordered!

Key correspondences included in this drink are:

ELDERBERRY. Elderberry is associated with magickal workings involving protection from psychic and emotional attack, protection from energy vampirism, spirit work, spirit communication, wisdom, clarity, cleansing and rebalancing.

LEMON. This citrus helps remove unwanted energies that may be blocking your path to success. It is used to cleanse, provide spiritual openings, purify and remove all blockages.

INGREDIENTS

★ 2 tbsp elderberry juice or syrup (or substitute with equal parts blueberry and blackberry juice as these berries carry immense protective properties)

★ 2 tbsp vodka

★ 2 tbsp freshly squeezed lemon juice

★ 1 tbsp sweetener of your choice

★ ½ tsp grated fresh ginger

★ 150ml/5fl oz/ scant ⅔ cup soda water

★ Ice cubes

Magickal Garnish

★ 3 elderberries

RITUAL

PRIOR TO DRINKING THIS POTION, TAKE A STEAMY SHOWER OR BATH FOR AT LEAST 30 MINS, CALLING ON THE POWER OF WATER TO ALLOW THE STEAM TO OPEN YOUR AIRWAYS AND CLEANSE YOUR BODY OF ANY IMPURITIES.

METHOD

★ Add all the ingredients to a tall serving glass filled with ice. Stir well.

★ Garnish with elderberries and enjoy!

RENEWAL

Let's keep it one hundred. Maybe we tried a few too many witchy cocktails last night, or "tested" one too many recipes from the For the Coven chapter (were those servings for 4 people? Oops!).

No matter what went down last night, this is the hangover elixir your body has been craving. It's also perfect for those times when you have gone on a spell bender and need some powerful magickal recovery. There isn't a hangover alive that can withstand the powerful presence of coconut water and cleansing cranberry. This combo will get you back on your feet and into your seat of power in no time.

Key correspondences included in this drink are:

COCONUT WATER. Coconut is associated with allure, confidence, diversity, flexibility, protection, psychic awareness, purification and spirituality.

CRANBERRY. Cranberries are associated with romance, warmth, cleansing, severing negative ties and promoting ambition.

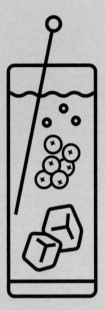

INGREDIENTS

★ 300ml/10½fl oz/ 1¼ cups coconut water

★ 180ml/6fl oz/ ¾ cup cranberry juice

★ Ice cubes

Magickal Garnish
★ Fresh cranberries

RITUAL

IN A CLEAR SEALED CONTAINER, ALLOW THE COCONUT WATER TO ABSORB LUNAR ENERGY FROM DIRECT MOONLIGHT FOR AT LEAST ONE HOUR. YOU CAN STORE COCONUT MOON WATER FOR UP TO A MAXIMUM THREE DAYS PRIOR TO USE.

METHOD

★ Pour both ingredients into a tall serving glass filled with ice and stir to mix.

★ Garnish with fresh cranberries and enjoy!

CLEANSING YOUR SPACE: WOKE SMOKE CLEANSING

Smudging, or sageing, has become the go-to cleansing ritual that many people use to clear away bad energy from their homes or their space. And while many companies and esoteric shops make a fortune selling "smudge sticks" and informing customers that for whatever ails them, smudging away bad energies is the key, they fail to realize two important factors: the ritual act of smudging is sacred and should only be done by indigenous North American folk, and that white sage is dangerously over-harvested.

Many people do not realize that the act of smudging is an important ritual for many indigenous people. Even the term "smudge" is intrinsically tied to this indigenous practice and should not be used by non-native people. Be sure to use the term "smoke-cleansing" instead if you are a non-native person cleansing yourself or your space with smoke through fumigation (smoke-cleansing an area) or suffumigation (smoke-cleansing oneself).

An article by Indigenous Corporate Training Inc., a Canadian organization that delivers anti-bias trainings, says that "Smudging is traditionally a ceremony for purifying or cleansing the soul of negative thoughts of a person or place", and that it is a term mostly originating from indigenous tribes in North America. So when non-native people burn sage to "smudge" their homes or other spaces, it can minimize the cultural importance of this ritual, and have a negative impact on how the herbs are grown. Even the way that indigenous folk harvest, consecrate and use the sage within their ritual is unique to their culture. It's not as simple as grabbing a white sage bundle, lighting it up and wafting the smoke with an eagle feather. (Obtaining eagle feathers is a federal crime in the US for non-natives.) I say this to emphasize how culturally tied the smudging ritual is to indigenous folk and how impossible, impractical, irresponsible and illegal it is for non-native people to appropriate and attempt to practice this ritual.

Instead, non-native people can learn to smoke-cleanse their spaces in ways that are culturally and ecologically sensitive. There are lots of ways to achieve the benefits of smudging by using more ethical practices, terminology and materials.

If you enjoy smoke-cleansing your space, fret not. You can do it in a culturally-conscious way. Smudging refers to a specific healing, cultural and spiritual practice, but smoke-cleansing can look a lot like smudging; it's just the

act of burning herbs, wood, incense or other safe-to-burn materials that possess cleansing properties. The smoke is then waved over the area you want to cleanse. The distinction is that the act of smoke-cleansing is not inherently spiritual or specific to a certain culture, unlike smudging.

Similar to white sage, palo santo ("holy wood" in Spanish) sticks have been getting more popular as a smoke-cleansing tool, but buying this Central and South American tree used by Amazonian tribes can also be harmful, in similar ways to sage. Palo santo has been added to the International Union for Conservation of Nature's list because over-harvesting can lead to its extinction, although the tree is not nearing extinction currently.

Personally, I like to use cedar bundles to smoke-cleanse. It leaves me feeling spiritually focused and relaxed and is such a lovely scent as well. And other materials, including lavender, pine, sweetgrass and cloves, can be burned safely.

prosperity

FINANCIAL SUCCESS

POTIONS

FINANCIAL SUCCESS POTIONS

The most highly requested spells, after those to attract love into one's life, are always financial gain. This inherent desire for financial success is deeply rooted in the belief that with it comes freedom to enjoy life the way it was always intended. The idea of being financially independent, or free from student loan debt, is understandably at the top of many minds right now.

These potions were created with that goal in mind: to attract financial success in order for you to be at your happiest. While these aren't "get rich quick" potion recipes that will win you the lotto or jackpot while gambling in a casino, they will draw prosperity to you thanks to the associated correspondences in each draught.

It's important to note that with any ritual, the right mindset is key. There's something to be said about the power of visualization and incorporating as many senses as possible to fully immerse yourself in the new reality you're creating. That's why in the following recipes visualization is vital in the success and fun when creating them.

Before we begin, let's take a moment to first understand the intention behind why you are seeking a financial boon or increase in monetary gain. Are you saving for a new car and are only short a few hundred bucks? Do you want to get yourself a new gaming laptop? Maybe you'd just like to take a vacation and get away for a week to refocus on what's truly important to you? Take some time to understand your reasons to increase your profits, as well as specifics in the total amount you'd like to see come your way. The more clear and concise you can be, the better!

For vegan substitutes please see page 28.

CORRESPONDENCES

INCENSE

dragon's blood, frankincense, mastic, palaginia, pepper

CRYSTALS TO WORK WITH FOR MONEY SPELLS

agate, amazonite, citrine, emerald, green jade, green aventurine, green moss agate, pyrite, clear quartz, rose quartz

DAYS OF THE WEEK FOR MONEY SPELLS

Thursday, Sunday

PLANETS FOR MONEY SPELLS

Jupiter, Sun

ZODIAC SIGNS FOR MONEY SPELLS

Taurus, Capricorn, Virgo

MOON PHASES FOR MONEY SPELLS

New Moon, Full Moon

SECURE THE BAG

Whether you work the nine-to-five grind or are hustling to become a self-started entrepreneur, we all could benefit from seeing our bank account stretch a bit further. This magickal concoction, flecked with gold, will reward your endeavors and hardworking mentality to bring you additional boons of success. It's time to secure the bag!

Key correspondences included in this drink are:

BERGAMOT. The flavor of Earl Grey tea comes from bergamot, a small orange that is usually green in color and has a lovely fragrance.

CINNAMON. Goldschläger is a Swiss cinnamon schnapps that is clear with very thin yet visible flakes of edible gold floating in it. Cinnamon is associated with success in all areas of life, predominantly with love and financial success. Cinnamon has the ability to draw money, victory and success your way while also being able to speed up spell results so they manifest more quickly.

EGGS. Eggs are symbolic wombs that internalize your desires. They are used in manifestation spells and magickal workings for this reason.

ORANGE. This citrus is in the simple syrup in the form of orange blossom honey, orange zest and its juice. Orange can be used to summon luck and to manifest prosperity.

INGREDIENTS

★ 2½ tbsp Goldschläger

★ 3½ tbsp strong, cold Earl Grey tea

★ 2 tbsp freshly squeezed lemon juice

★ 2 tbsp pasteurized liquid egg white

★ 1 tbsp orange simple syrup (see below)

★ Ice cubes

For the orange simple syrup:

★ 180ml/6fl oz/ ¾ cup water

★ Zest of 1 orange

★ 2 tbsp freshly squeezed orange juice

★ 120ml/4fl oz/ ½ cup orange blossom honey

Magickal Garnish

★ Draw a dollar sign with orange syrup on the inside of the glass prior to pouring in the drink. Visualize the precise amount you desire and the reasons you want it.

RITUAL

WHILE PREPARING THIS DRINK ALLOW THE SERVING GLASS TO REST ON TOP OF AN UNFOLDED DOLLAR BILL. WHILE YOU POUR THE POTION INTO THE GLASS, GENTLY REMOVE THE DOLLAR BILL WHILE SAYING: "MAY PROSPERITY FIND ITS WAY TO ME, AS I WILL SO MOTE IT BE."

METHOD

★ Make the orange simple syrup by bringing the water to the boil in a saucepan over a medium heat, then add the orange zest, orange juice and honey. Turn the heat down to low and simmer for 7 mins, stirring to dissolve the honey, then cool and strain before bottling. This will keep in the refrigerator for up to 1 week.

★ To make the cocktail, add all the ingredients including the ice cubes to a cocktail shaker and mix well until frothy.

★ Strain into your prepared glass.

IT MAKES CENTS

This boozy blackberry lemonade will brighten your day and allow for a sunny disposition when contemplating your next financial move. Allow the power of lemons to blast away any troublesome thoughts and obstacles that may be blocking potential opportunities from coming your way. With a clear head and bright disposition, the next step you take will just make cents.

Key correspondences included in this drink are:

BLACKBERRY. Blackberries are used in workings of healing, protection and money magick. They are sacred to Brighid, the goddess of spring, healing, creative arts and protection. The leaves and berries are said to attract wealth and healing.

MINT. This herb is known to draw customers to a business and promote financial success. Dried mint leaves are used in prosperity spells to bring wealth to the caster.

LEMON. This citrus helps remove unwanted energies that may be blocking your path to success. It is used to cleanse, provide spiritual openings, purify and remove all blockages.

INGREDIENTS

★ 150g/5oz/ heaped ½ cup blackberries

★ 2 tsp sweetener of your choice

★ 3 sprigs fresh mint

★ 6 tbsp limoncello (or lemon-flavored vodka), or 6 tbsp sparkling water

★ Juice of 3 lemons

★ Crushed ice

★ Extra sparkling water, optional

Magickal Garnish

★ Sugared lemon slice

★ A few blackberries

★ Fresh mint leaves

RITUAL

PRIOR TO MAKING THIS MAGICKAL DRINK, ALLOW YOUR LEMONS TO SOAK IN THE SUNSHINE FOR AT LEAST THREE HOURS ON ANY DAY BEFORE JUICING. THIS CAN BE DONE BY RESTING YOUR LEMONS ON YOUR WINDOWSILL OR IN YOUR BACKYARD. FOR BEST RESULTS, CREATE THIS POTION ON A SUNDAY AND TAKE YOUR FIRST SIP FACING EASTWARD (THE DIRECTION THE SUN RISES).

METHOD

★ In a large bowl, muddle (mash) the blackberries with a fork.

★ Add your sweetener and fresh mint to the blackberry mixture and mash to release essential oils from the mint.

★ Add the limoncello, if using, or sparkling water, and the lemon juice, then stir to combine.

★ Transfer to an easy-to-pour container.

★ Pour the potion into a short serving glass filled with crushed ice.

★ Serve garnished with a sugared lemon slice, a few blackberries and mint leaves. Top with more sparkling water, if desired.

LADY LUCK'S KISS

Some people just seem to be a wealth magnet. Everywhere they go, happy coincidences follow them – from stumbling across a substantial amount of money on the ground to receiving free perks that save them money in the long run. It's almost as if they received Lady Luck's kiss and she's blessed the ground they walk on. It's time for that someone to be you. With every sip you take of this mint chocolatey drink, imagine becoming a magnet for wealth and prosperity. Now that's something to drink to!

Key correspondences included in this drink are:

CHOCOLATE. Dark chocolate as well as cacao nibs have been associated with drawing prosperity to the caster due to their rich and earthy nature.

MINT. This herb is known to draw customers to a business and promote financial success. Dried mint leaves are used in prosperity spells to bring wealth to the caster.

INGREDIENTS

- ★ Ice cubes
- ★ 2 tbsp Baileys Irish Cream
- ★ 2 tbsp crème de menthe liqueur
- ★ 2 tbsp whole milk/half and half
- ★ Squirty cream

Magickal Garnish
- ★ Dark chocolate gold coin

RITUAL

WITH EVERY SIP YOU TAKE OF THIS MINT CHOCOLATEY DRINK, IMAGINE BECOMING A MAGNET FOR WEALTH, PROSPERITY AND GOOD FORTUNE.

METHOD

- ★ Fill a cocktail shaker with ice.
- ★ Add all the ingredients (except the squirty cream), cover and shake well.
- ★ Strain into a martini glass.
- ★ Finish with a squirt of whipped cream and garnish the glass with a dark chocolate gold coin.

GET THAT BREAD

Imagine what life would be like living like the upper crust. Every day you'd be a success story rolling in dough. Okay, I'll stop with the bread puns now. Seriously, though, life is crumby when all your money goes to your needs and never your wants. It's the pleasures in the life that make life worth living. So let's toast to living our best life and getting that bread!

Key correspondences included in this drink are:

LEMON. This citrus helps remove unwanted energies that may be blocking your path to success. It is used to cleanse, provide spiritual openings, purify and remove all blockages.

ALMOND. Amaretto is an almond-flavored liqueur. Almonds are used in magickal workings of protection and luck. They are thought to relieve loneliness and assist in achieving success in your goals to attain friendship or love. Almonds attract luck and success in all forms.

BEER. Beer is associated with the element of Earth. It is useful in spells to promote health, draw success, and aid in making the drink more prosperous.

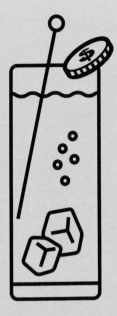

INGREDIENTS

★ Ice cubes
★ 3½ tbsp light beer (like a pale ale)
★ 1½ tbsp Amaretto liqueur
★ 2 tbsp sweetener of your choice
★ 1½ tbsp freshly squeezed lemon juice
★ 125ml/4fl oz/ ½ cup lemon-lime soda

Magickal Garnish
★ Gold chocolate coin

RITUAL

AFTER CLEANSING AND PROTECTING YOUR SPACE, CALL UPON THE ENERGY OF LADY LUCK TO ASSIST YOU IN THIS RITUAL: "LADY LUCK, I BESEECH YOU. ALLOW ME TO WALK YOUR GOLDEN PATH SO TRUE." THEN PUCKER UP AND PLANT THREE KISSES AROUND THE EXTERIOR OF YOUR SERVING GLASS PRIOR TO CREATING YOUR POTION.

METHOD

★ In a tall serving glass filled with ice, mix together the beer, Amaretto, sweetener and lemon juice.

★ Top with the lemon-lime soda, garnish with a chocolate coin, and enjoy!

PROSPERI-TEA

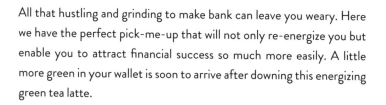

All that hustling and grinding to make bank can leave you weary. Here we have the perfect pick-me-up that will not only re-energize you but enable you to attract financial success so much more easily. A little more green in your wallet is soon to arrive after downing this energizing green tea latte.

Key correspondences included in this drink are:

GREEN TEA. Matcha is made from powdered green tea leaves. Green tea is associated with health, love, passion, energy, cleansing and money-drawing spells.

RICE MILK. Rice resonates with the energy of the earth and is associated with spells for blessing, money, prosperity, fertility and protection. Rice is also associated with magickal workings for wealth, security and attaining treasure.

INGREDIENTS

★ 80ml/2½fl oz/ ⅓ cup rice milk

★ 1 tsp matcha powder

★ 4 tbsp boiling water

★ Sweetener of your choice, to taste

Magickal Garnish

★ Matcha powder symbol stencil

RITUAL

A) PREPARE WITH A PYRITE STONE IN YOUR POCKET OR NEARBY. PYRITE ASSISTS IN DRAWING SUCCESS.

B) STENCIL A SYMBOL WITH MATCHA TO REPRESENT YOUR DESIRE. A HEART FOR SUCCESS IN LOVE, A DOLLAR SIGN FOR PROSPERITY, OR A SMILEY FACE FOR GENERAL SUCCESS AND HAPPINESS. WHISPER YOUR DESIRE ALOUD UNTIL THE STENCIL IS COMPLETE.

METHOD

★ In a small saucepan over a low heat, bring the rice milk to a bare simmer. Place the matcha powder in a heatproof cup. Slowly whisk in the boiling water, then the rice milk. You can tip the cup slightly to help create more foam.

★ Add sweetener to taste.

★ Stencil your matcha symbol on to the top of your potion.

beauty

BEAUTY

POTIONS

BEAUTY POTIONS

Beauty is in the eye of the beholder, or it might be in the hands of the beauty-industry corporate overlords. Either way, beauty can sometimes feel like an intangible leveraging factor with the power to make or break your success in a number of ways. Whereas personality is inherent to who you are, beauty (at least outer beauty) is malleable.

If you wear the right look, then you can get a job at your favorite clothing brand. Style yourself in the right aesthetic and you can score a second date. This inherent belief that beauty and attractiveness is at arm's reach is the underpinning of our beauty and fashion industries. It's the same belief that tells us internet-famous likeability is attainable if we just buy the right skincare line, new bag, etc. That if you can just find that matching foundation, you can have the world in the palm of your hand.

But there's something to be said for the power of inner beauty and its transformative abilities. Every witch knows inner beauty trumps outer any day of the week, because it's inherent to who we are. Loving who you are instills confidence that permeates throughout your entire being. It makes you radiant and attracts those around you like moths to a flame.

Self-love, my friends, is the true barometer of beauty. Don't believe me? Next time you're in a room full of people, take a look around and see which people are at the center of attention. It'll likely be the happiest, most self-confident individual there. They may not be the most well dressed or have TikTok or Instagram model looks but there's something about them that blows the others away.

It's time to drink up some beauty potions that will turn any caterpillar into a butterfly. At the very least it'll make you smile a little bit more, and the world just loves to see you smile.

For vegan substitutes please see page 28.

CORRESPONDENCES

INCENSE
heather, lady's mantle, lemon, orange, rose, strawberry, violet

PLANET FOR BEAUTY SPELLS
Venus

CRYSTALS TO WORK WITH FOR BEAUTY SPELLS
amber, aquamarine, jade, onyx, opal, red jasper, rose quartz, topaz

ZODIAC SIGNS FOR BEAUTY SPELLS
Leo, Scorpio, Aries, Sagittarius

DAY OF THE WEEK FOR BEAUTY SPELLS
Friday

MOON PHASE FOR BEAUTY SPELLS
Waxing Moon

MORNING GLOW

For those looking for a morning wake-up-and-glow potion, this is the one for you. This recipe uses a magickal infusion of lavender and jasmine, and it's sure to leave you feeling energized and radiant (thanks to the power of green tea). Brew yourself a batch to start your week off right, you stunner!

Key correspondences included in this drink are:

LAVENDER. The scent of lavender allegedly attracts sexual interest from others while simultaneously sharpening the wits of the wearer.

HONEY. Like other sweeteners, honey has long been associated with a deep, resonating connection, enduring love and prosperity. There's a reason the sweetest part of a relationship is called the honeymoon phase.

JASMINE. Jasmine is associated with sensuality and spiritual workings alike and is commonly used in spells of love, divination and beauty. It's also used in love-drawing magick and is said to attract spiritually pure love (as opposed to spicy flings).

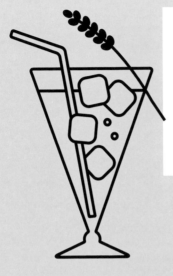

INGREDIENTS

- ★ 250ml/8½fl oz/ 1 cup water
- ★ 2 jasmine green tea bags
- ★ 2 tbsp orange blossom honey
- ★ 7 lavender flower buds
- ★ Ice cubes
- ★ 1½ tbsp whiskey

Magickal Garnish
- ★ Lemon slices
- ★ Dried jasmine flowers, optional
- ★ Dried lavender flowers, optional

RITUAL

DRINK AND REPEAT THE CHARM "I BLOOM, THEY SWOON" SEVEN TIMES PRIOR TO GAZING INTO ANY MIRROR.

METHOD

★ Bring the water to the boil in a saucepan over a medium-low heat. Add the honey and stir until it has dissolved. Leave to cool for 3 mins.

★ Add the tea bags and the lavender flower buds to the saucepan, then stir and let steep for 3 mins. Strain the mixture and discard the used tea bags and lavender.

★ Transfer the tea to a container and refrigerate until cool, about 13 mins.

★ Fill a serving glass with ice. Pour in the whiskey and then the tea (there might be some tea left over). Garnish with lemon slices, dried jasmine flowers and dried lavender flowers, if using.

LOOKS TO KILL

There are moments you want to stop people dead in their tracks with your style and grace. If you're looking to make an entrance that will leave them breathless, then take a swig of this killer potion. Caution: consuming this brew will not only put all eyes on you but will make them bow to you.

Key correspondences included in this drink are:

HONEY. Like other sweeteners, honey has long been associated with a deep, resonating connection, enduring love and prosperity. There's a reason the sweetest part of a relationship is called the honeymoon phase.

ROSE WATER. Rose water has a variety of uses, such as being a protective agent against the evil eye or those jealous of you. It brings love and happiness to your life and can be worn for general protection and good luck.

ROSE QUARTZ. A phenomenal crystal of universal love. It works wonders for all matters of the heart and assists in workings to encourage unconditional love, self-love, romantic love, friendship, platonic love and every facet of love itself.

INGREDIENTS

- ★ 2 tbsp gin
- ★ 2 tbsp freshly squeezed lemon juice
- ★ 4 tbsp rose simple syrup (see below)
- ★ Ice cubes
- ★ Splash of soda water/club soda

Rose simple syrup:
- ★ 240ml/8fl oz/ 1 cup water
- ★ 350g/12oz/ 1 cup honey
- ★ 1 tsp rose extract

- ★ Rose petals (optional)

Magickal Garnish
- ★ Twist of lemon peel
- ★ Sugared rose petals (To make: coat flower petals in a thin layer of egg white wash, then dip them into caster/ granulated sugar and leave them to dry for a few hours.)

RITUAL

GET DRESSED TO THE NINES WHILE MAKING THIS POTION. TAKE THE TIME TO ADORN YOURSELF SO THAT YOU FEEL LIKE THE GOD OR GODDESS YOU TRULY ARE. YOU ARE REQUIRED TO STRUT AROUND BEFORE, DURING AND AFTER CONSUMING THIS BREW.

METHOD

★ Put the water and honey into a small saucepan over a medium-low heat and simmer until the honey has dissolved. Leave to cool for 7 mins alongside a rose quartz crystal you have charged with the intention of being the most badass witch in existence. Then add the rose water extract.

★ If you're serving right away, you could add rose petals to the syrup for beautiful presentation. Any leftover syrup can be stored in the refrigerator for up to 1 week.

★ To make the cocktail, add the gin, lemon juice and syrup to a cocktail shaker filled with ice and shake for 30 secs. Strain into a short glass with a large ice cube and add a splash of soda water/club soda. Garnish with the lemon peel and a petal.

EYE CANDY

Do you want to become aesthetically pleasing to the senses of everyone that crosses your path? Or serve the world a feast for the eyes just by walking into a room? Maybe you want to catch the eye of the special someone you'd like to be sweet on you. Then get a whiff of this scrumptious magickal cocktail that will infuse you with an aura of sweetness and leave them salivating for more.

Key correspondences included in this drink are:

VODKA. Many modern versions of vodka are made with fruit or sugar. Vodka has been associated with transformation, strength and courage, and it uplifts you.

ORANGE. This vibrant citrus can be used to summon luck and to manifest prosperity.

CANDY. Lore behind candy is typically based on the idea that it's a tool for appeasing energies outside ourselves which will then work in our favor. It's also used as an offering to remove obstacles in your way and to sweeten the path so success can find its way to you.

INGREDIENTS

- ★ 2 tbsp whipped cream vodka (or regular vodka)
- ★ 2 tbsp whole milk/half and half
- ★ 2 tbsp fruit punch/tropical fruit juice

- ★ 100ml/3½fl oz/ scant ½ cup orange juice
- ★ Splash of lemon-lime soda

Magickal Garnish
- ★ Pink Starburst or other pink candy

RITUAL

WHISTLE THE SWEETEST SONG YOU CAN THINK OF WHILE CREATING THIS POTION. LET THE MUSIC LIFT YOUR SPIRITS AND BRING A SMILE TO YOUR FACE.

METHOD

★ Mix the vodka, milk/half and half and fruit punch/tropical fruit juice in a tall serving glass.

★ Stir in the orange juice and top with a splash of lemon-lime soda.

★ Garnish with pink Starburst candy or other pink candy on the rim of the glass.

FOUNTAIN OF YOUTH

Imagine waking up feeling well rested. In today's world, that goal can feel out of reach on a daily basis. This night-time potion will refresh your body, mind and soul. Pair this routine with the Morning Glow brew (see page 82) and you'll have a one-two combo that'll make anyone whose gaze falls on you weak at the knees.

Key correspondences included in this drink are:

LEMON. This citrus helps remove unwanted energies that may be blocking your path to success. It is used to cleanse, provide spiritual openings, purify and remove all blockages.

HONEY. Like other sweeteners, honey has long been associated with a deep, resonating connection, enduring love and prosperity. There's a reason the sweetest part of a relationship is called the honeymoon phase.

BUTTERFLY PEA FLOWERS. This magickal plant has the power to reduce inflammation and increase vitality. The tea has been shown to possess moderate anxiolytic and anti-depressive effects.

INGREDIENTS

★ 125ml/4fl oz/ ½ cup boiling water

★ 10 butterfly pea flowers

★ 2 tbsp honey

★ Ice cubes

★ 4 tbsp lemon juice

★ 2 tbsp lemon-lime soda

Magickal Garnish
★ Lemon slice

★ 3 butterfly pea flowers

RITUAL

AS YOU POUR THE LEMON JUICE INTO THE BLUE POTION, IMAGINE A BRIGHT PINK LIGHT FILLING YOU UP, INFUSING YOUR BODY WITH RADIANT, GLOWING VITAL ENERGY.

METHOD

★ Create a butterfly pea flower tea infusion by pouring the hot water into a mug over the butterfly pea flowers. Stir in the honey until dissolved and allow the infusion to cool for about 3 mins.

★ Strain the infusion into a tall, heatproof glass filled with ice.

★ Add the lemon juice for color-changing magick.

★ Top with the soda, garnish and enjoy!

CORRESPONDENCES AND CELESTIAL SYNCHRONICITY

Agriculture is one of humanity's oldest sciences. Originally herbs, fruits, vegetables and the like were harvested and collected following lunar cycles and phases. Human society would look to the heavens to decipher instruction and meaning within the constellations and celestial bodies. Using this information, they had then determined that universal energies existed which could be categorized based on planetary association. From that came the organization of magickal timing based on planetary associations. This is how planetary days and hours were created.

Many magickal-minded folks still hold to the idea to time a spell following planetary associations. It is believed that if the working is done during a particular planetary day, and on a particular hour of astrological house timings, it will add an additional layer of potency and success to the magickal work.

While I have found this to be true through my own experience, I also know that timing comes second to necessity if there is an emergency that needs attention, for example, you are feeling jinxed and need to create a cleansing ritual, or you're coming down with something and you need to create a health potion. My priority always leans toward necessity over waiting to time a spell based on planetary correspondence.

To hammer this point home even more, imagine that you've started to feel unsafe in your home or sacred space. Every time you're home it feels eerie, unsettling, and you swear negativity has infiltrated. Do you really think it prudent to wait until Saturday or Monday to complete a cleansing and protection ritual? Of course not! You should perform one right away, the instant you feel things are out of whack.

Harvesting and collecting herbs should follow the same strategy. If you have a need for herbal correspondences, like bay leaves for a wish spell you'd like to perform on Thursday, then wait until Thursday to collect the bay leaves and perform your magickal working. If you have a dire need to perform a protection spell and are looking for black salt and chilli peppers, then head to your nearest food market and pick them up right away! Do not linger and postpone because the planetary day or hours aren't aligned; your safety and well-being are always the number one priority.

PSYCHIC POWER

POTIONS

PSYCHIC POWER POTIONS

Psychic abilities are incredibly fascinating, and bolstering what we already have is as simple as drinking down a lovely little brew. Think about what it might be like to grow your clairsenses (magickal senses). You could see what's occurring across vast distances in real time, hear the thoughts of those around you, feel the emotions others have experienced long ago in a particular location, or be struck with sudden knowledge and understanding of a question you're sure a minute ago would've stumped you. These abilities aren't gifts for the chosen but reside within each one of us, dulled from disuse and waiting for the chance to grow stronger.

The best time to brew a batch of potions for psychic power is during the witching hour, at 3am, but since most of us have class or work in the morning, that may not be feasible. Instead let's just time our brews by the light of the moon. Who's ready for some moon magick? There's nothing like some lunar energy to invigorate the mind and empower the psychic senses. The following brews are sure to deliver you into a trance-state of bliss that'll allow you to enhance your psychic power.

It's time to venture inwards to unlock your psychic abilities in clairvoyance (magickal sight), clairaudience (magickal hearing), clairsentience (magickal feeling) and claircognizance (magickal knowing). We figure that clairgustance and clairalience, the senses of taste and smell, will be delighted and enhanced naturally just through creating these concoctions.

For vegan substitutes please see page 28.

CORRESPONDENCES

INCENSE

cedar, cinnamon, dragon's blood, frankincense lavender, myrrh

CRYSTALS TO WORK WITH FOR PSYCHIC POWER SPELLS

amethyst, angelite, apatite, aquamarine, azurite, beryl, calcite, clear quartz, emerald, jet, lapis lazuli, malachite, moonstone, opal, ruby, sapphire, smokey quartz, tiger's eye, tourmaline

DAY OF THE WEEK FOR PSYCHIC POWER SPELLS

Monday

PLANETS FOR PSYCHIC POWER SPELLS

Moon, Neptune

ZODIAC SIGNS FOR PSYCHIC POWER SPELLS

Cancer, Capricorn, Pisces, Scorpio

MOON PHASES FOR PSYCHIC POWER SPELLS

New Moon, Full Moon

THIRD–EYE ELIXIR

This third-eye elixir is meant to enhance the vision of how you'd like your future to unfold. We could all use a bit more insight into our decision-making, and this potion not only provides that in spades but also enhances your clairvoyant abilities. Become more than meets the eye by taking self-predicted steps toward the future you've already envisioned.

Try to brew this potion during the night of a New Moon to plant the seeds for your success, and allow your vision of your ideal self to take root. Extra magickal points go to those who adorn themselves with shades of purple and who hold an amethyst during their visualization.

Key correspondences included in this drink are:

LAVENDER. The scent of lavender allegedly attracts sexual interest from others while simultaneously sharpening the wits of the wearer. Lavender tea is known to strengthen mental and psychic faculties.

LEMON. This citrus helps remove unwanted energies that may be blocking your path to success. It is used to cleanse, provide spiritual openings, purify and remove all blockages.

AMETHYST. This magickal stone is a semi-precious stone of power which specializes in happiness, psychic ability and peace.

INGREDIENTS

* ★ 2 tbsp vodka
* ★ 3½ tbsp freshly squeezed lemon juice
* ★ 3½ tbsp lavender syrup (see right)
* ★ Ice cubes

For the lavender syrup:
* ★ 240ml/8fl oz/ 1 cup water
* ★ 200g/7oz/ 1 cup caster/ granulated sugar
* ★ 1 tbsp dried lavender buds

Magickal Garnish
* ★ Lemon slice

RITUAL

IT IS IMPERATIVE YOU SPEAK ALOUD, FOR A MINIMUM OF NINE MINUTES, YOUR MOST PASSIONATE HOPES AND DREAMS. DO YOUR BEST TO SEE CLEARLY IN YOUR MIND'S EYE YOURSELF SUCCEEDING IN EVERY ENDEAVOR. CAPTURE THOSE ACHIEVEMENTS FULLY, WITH ALL YOUR SENSES.

METHOD

★ To make the lavender syrup: bring the water and sugar to the boil in a saucepan over a medium heat, stirring until the sugar dissolves. Remove from the heat, add the lavender buds and leave to infuse for 20 mins. Strain and allow to cool. Store any leftover syrup in a glass jar in the refrigerator. It will keep for a week.

★ To make the cocktail, put the vodka, lemon juice and lavender syrup into a cocktail shaker filled with ice and shake well.

★ Strain into a martini glass and garnish with a lemon slice.

ODE TO POWER

This is ideal for musicians, singers, writers and public speakers. If you have the gift of the gab or song, it's time to put it to work. An ode is a lyrical poem focused on a particular subject and elevated in the style of your liking. You'll be manifesting "An Ode to Claiming Personal Power"!

You are a gift to the world with something unique to offer. While this may sound like it belongs on an inspirational poster, the fact is it's true. You are the only you that exists right now, in this space and time. Own your power and let your voice boom with pride. For all those moments you held your tongue, the times you decided not to shine your brightest, it's time to take that power back and belt your desires to the world. Once you free yourself through song, written word or lyrical jaunt, the answers to achieving your goals will find you serendipitously in videos, music or casual conversation over the next few days.

Key correspondences included in this drink are:

PEPPERMINT. Used in matters of breaking bad habits, communication, divination, eloquence, intelligence, mental powers, psychic powers, self-improvement, study, travel and wisdom.

COCONUT. Associated with workings to enhance allure, confidence, flexibility, protection, psychic awareness, purification, spirituality.

FLAXSEED. Associated with workings to enhance beauty, healing, protection, money, and psychic enhancement.

INGREDIENTS

★ 2 tbsp chocolate vodka (or regular vodka)

★ 1 tbsp peppermint schnapps

★ 1½ tbsp Rum Chata cream liqueur

★ 4 tbsp coconut milk

★ 4 tbsp flaxseed milk

★ Ice cubes

Magickal Garnish

★ Crushed charmed peppermint candies or mint chocolates

★ Mint leaves

RITUAL

PLACE PEPPERMINT CANDIES OR PEPPERMINT CHOCOLATES IN THE LIGHT OF A FULL MOON AND WHISPER OR SING YOUR SECRETS THAT HAVE BEEN HALTING YOUR PROGRESS. CRUSH THE CANDIES TO RELEASE AND DISPERSE THE STORED ENERGY, THEN LINE THE RIM OF YOUR SERVING GLASS TO GARNISH.

METHOD

★ Pour all the ingredients into a cocktail shaker filled with ice.

★ Shake well.

★ Strain into a tall serving glass that has been prepared as described in the ritual, and fill with ice.

★ Garnish with charmed peppermint candies or peppermint chocolates and fresh mint leaves.

DÉJÀ VU JUICE

Sometimes during deep conversations with others we sync up. It's like we sense each other's emotions, even physical or emotional pain. Many of us are clairsentient without being aware of it. Those occasions in life when you're at your front door and get a strong "gut" feeling – positive or negative – about a place you plan to go, or someone you plan to see; this emotional energy can help steer us in the right direction.

Déjà vu is the feeling of having experienced reality already. That emotional tug like we're in the right place at the right time with the right people can set off déjà vu, like a spiritual pat on the back for figuring out how to arrive at a good destination. Being sensitive in this way allows us to be better communicators and get a third-person perspective on life. Déjà Vu Juice will heighten your senses to make you a magickal feeler. You'll connect more easily with others, have greater empathy and walk the right path for you.

Key correspondences included in this drink are:

<u>CINNAMON</u>. Useful for lifting or increasing power, psychic abilities and spiritual connectedness.

<u>NUTMEG</u>. Tied to magickal workings of good luck. It is also burned to aid in meditation, and to stimulate or increase psychic powers.

<u>ALLSPICE</u>. This magickal spice is associated with healing. You can burn allspice to attract both good luck and money.

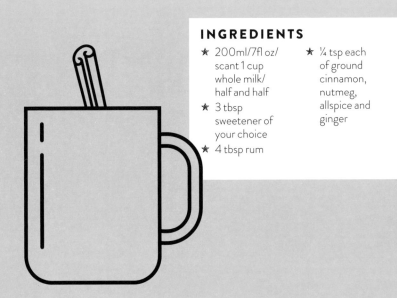

INGREDIENTS

★ 200ml/7fl oz/ scant 1 cup whole milk/ half and half

★ 3 tbsp sweetener of your choice

★ 4 tbsp rum

★ ¼ tsp each of ground cinnamon, nutmeg, allspice and ginger

RITUAL

MIX THE SPICES TOGETHER AND PLACE IN A COVERED GLASS CONTAINER. PLACE THE CONTAINER IN THE LIGHT OF A WAXING MOON. USE THE SPICES WITHIN THE NEXT 3 DAYS.

METHOD

★ In a saucepan over a low heat, gently warm the milk/half and half. Add the sweetener and stir until it dissolves.

★ Add in the spices and whisk to combine.

★ Whisk in the rum, then pour into a serving glass or mug. Enjoy!

BACK FROM THE FUTURE

Have you ever wished you had knowledge of people or events that you would not normally have knowledge about? Allow your psychic abilities in claircognizance to flourish and this will allow truths to simply pop into your mind from out of nowhere.

The most common form of claircognizance is premonition: a forewarning of something that will happen in the future. It can also be a useful tool to increase your confidence in projects you're working on, for college or job applications, or to understand the outcome of personal relationships. Using your intuition will empower you with confidence that you're well on the way to the success you're after.

Key correspondences included in this drink are:

ABSINTHE. The wormwood within absinthe stimulates and enhances psychic abilities.

LIME. This citrus helps remove unwanted energies that may be blocking your path to success. It is used to cleanse, provide spiritual openings, purify and remove all blockages.

ORANGE. The high-energy scent of oranges is said to communicate with spiritual energies, allowing you to connect to higher planes for answers you seek and for guidance.

INGREDIENTS

★ 1 tbsp absinthe

★ 2 tbsp freshly squeezed lime juice

★ 2 tbsp sweetener of your choice

★ 125ml/4fl oz/ ½ cup water

★ Ice cubes

Magickal Garnish

★ Slices of orange peel

RITUAL

DRINK THIS POTION WHILE FACING WEST AND CALLING IN THE ENERGY OF THE ELEMENT OF WATER TO GUIDE YOU WHILE DIVING INTO YOUR FUTURE.

METHOD

★ Add all the ingredients to a tall serving glass filled with ice and stir to mix.

★ Garnish with twists of orange peel.

★ Enjoy!

DREAM

POTIONS

DREAM POTIONS

Dreams have the ability to transcend time, space and reality. It is within our dreams that we have the capability to escape the mundane world, plumb the depths of our emotions, discover roots to our most coveted belief systems and understand what it is that we truly desire. Sometimes our dreams can even surprise us and reveal shocking insights we might be unprepared to face, like the secret crush you've been harboring for your classmate or co-worker, oops!

Understanding what we dream, as well as goal-setting to make our wildest dreams a possibility, are all within our reach. We just have to take a step back, remind our mind who's in charge and slip into a restful sleep full of enlightenment. With the reclaiming of our willpower, we'll be able to focus our mind to bring our dreams closer to us.

There are many facets to a dream: a scenario conjured up as we sleep, a life's goal we yearn to reach or a fantasy we wish can be played out. All of these ideas are seeded with the power of our will, and with a little tweaking of our mindset combined with some helpful correspondences, you may have all you've ever imagined within the palm of your hand.

The following potions work to aid in dream recall, attaining your dreams, getting a full night's rest and visiting dreamland in your waking state to bring your dreams into reality.

For vegan substitutes please see page 28.

CORRESPONDENCES

INCENSE
bay, cedar, anise, clary sage,
jasmine, lavender, lemongrass,
rosemary

CRYSTALS TO WORK
WITH FOR DREAM SPELLS
agate, amethyst, angel
phantom quartz, clear quartz,
blue calcite, dream quartz,
iolite, moonstone,
smoky quartz, stilbite

DAY OF THE WEEK FOR
DREAM SPELLS
Monday

PLANET FOR DREAM
SPELLS
Moon

ZODIAC SIGNS
FOR DREAM SPELLS
Pisces, Cancer, Scorpio

MOON PHASE
FOR DREAM SPELLS
Waning Moon

FORGET ME NOT

Have you ever been having a really good dream only to get startled awake by your alarm, or some other jarring noise, with every glorious detail of that very nice dream slipping away? It happens to the best of us, even those keeping faithful dream journals. The reason dream recall and memory post-sleep can be faulty at times has to do with low levels of neurochemicals that assist in storing memories, namely norepinephrine, during phases of REM (rapid eye movement) sleep.

Biochemistry aside, it'd be nice to linger over the details of our dreams whenever we'd like. Especially if, in the case of a prophetic dream that seems like a warning, recovering all the facts and details may prove useful in the future. This potion allows for exactly that, to relive our reveries and linger in our dream state for a bit longer before returning to the mortal plane.

Key correspondences included in this drink are:

FORGET–ME–NOT. This purple tea made from the loose buds of the *myosotis sylvatica* flower has a mild, grassy flavor. It promotes a restful sleep and also keeps important thoughts close to mind.

COFFEE. Coffee correspondences can speed up spells, remove nightmares when a bag of beans is hung over your bed, and cleanse a space when used in floor washes or spray. Coffee contains high amounts of caffeine, which has been shown to boost memory.

INGREDIENTS

- ★ 125ml/4fl oz/ ½ cup hot coffee
- ★ 125ml/4fl oz/ ½ cup steamed milk or non-dairy alternative
- ★ ½ tsp forget-me-not flower buds
- ★ Sweetener of your choice, to taste

Magickal Garnish
- ★ Forget-me-not flowers

RITUAL

AS YOU WAKE, TRY NOT TO MOVE. RELAX INTO A COMFORTABLE STATE AND TRY TO RECALL THE END OF YOUR DREAM AND WORK BACKWARDS. JOT DOWN AS MUCH AS YOU CAN. THEN, GET UP AND PREPARE THE POTION, BESEECHING THE LUNAR ENERGIES AND THE ELEMENT OF WATER TO HELP YOU REMEMBER YOUR DREAM.

METHOD

- ★ Brew the coffee and pour into a serving mug.
- ★ Pour the steamed milk into a separate mug, add the forget-me-not buds and allow to steep for 3 mins.
- ★ Strain the steamed milk infusion into your coffee and sweeten to taste, stirring. Garnish with forget-me-not flowers.
- ★ Allow each powerful sip to extract and call forth details of your dream.

DOZING DAIQUIRI

There's nothing like kicking your shoes off and relaxing after a long or stressful week. But with all that tension you may find it difficult to get the restful sleep you deserve. This sleep-inducing potion will fill you up with comforting magick and whisk you off to dreamland.

This potion is perfect for the type of person who wants help hitting the hay without having to down an herbal sleepytime tea. If you're looking for something substantial, creamy and delicious, then this concoction will take you from night owl to sleepyhead before you get to the bottom of the glass.

Key correspondences included in this drink are:

BANANA. This fruit has the potency to induce sleep, promote a painless sleep, induce dreams, guard against depression, moderate blood sugar levels and reduce the possibility of cramps.

CHERRY. Cherries have the power to aid in divination workings, induce sleep, induce dreams and promote healthy eyesight. They also act as an anti-inflammatory.

OATMEAL/OAT MILK. Oats are a hearty grain that aid in inducing dreams, as well as grounding, prosperity, beauty, healing and health magick.

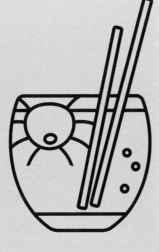

INGREDIENTS

★ 2½ tbsp light rum

★ 1 tbsp triple sec

★ 1 banana, peeled

★ 3 tbsp freshly squeezed lime juice

★ 8 maraschino cherries

★ 1 tsp maraschino cherry liquid

★ 2 scoops of vanilla oat milk ice cream (or other oat milk-based frozen dessert)

Magickal Garnish

★ Maraschino cherry and 8 cherry stems to represent a spider catching evil in its web

RITUAL

CALL ON THE AID OF SPIDERS TO ENSNARE ALL THAT IS TROUBLESOME FOR RESTFUL SLEEP: "SPIDER, OH SPIDER, WEAVE A DREAM SO FINE, ENSNARE AND TRAP EVIL WHICH IS UNKIND. SPIDER, DEAR SPIDER, SPIN ME OFF TO SLEEP, NO MORE STRESS, EASE MY CHEST AS I SLIP INTO BLESSED PEACE."

METHOD

★ Put all the ingredients into a blender.

★ Blend on low speed for a few secs, then at high speed until smooth.

★ Pour into a serving glass, then garnish with the maraschino cherry spider (1 cherry studded with 8 cherry stems).

★ Drink and follow up with a glass of warm water before heading to bed!

SWEET DREAM LAND

This is a recipe that has been handed down through my maternal bloodline. It's a magickal potion that will aid in providing restful sleep when it is determined not to come. My family swears by this recipe and I've seen it work first-hand. It is potent, but you can brew it nightly to help with cases of severe insomnia.

Key correspondences included in this drink are:

GUANABANA LEAVES (OR LINDEN LEAVES). Guanabana, also called soursop or custard apple, is native to Africa and Brazil. This fruit as well as its leaves are used in powerful unblocking baths when one is oppressed by fate. It is also used in breaking bonds, contracts, friendships and bad habits and bringing balance back to the individual.

LEMON. This citrus helps remove unwanted energies that may be blocking your path to success. It is used to cleanse, provide spiritual openings, purify and remove all blockages.

HONEY. Like other sweeteners, honey has long been associated with a deep, resonating connection, enduring health, love and prosperity.

INGREDIENTS

* 5–6 guanabana leaves
* 200ml/7fl oz/ scant 1 cup boiling water
* 2 tbsp freshly squeezed lemon or lime juice
* 2 tbsp honey or other sweetener of your choice

Magickal Garnish
* Sliced lemon
* 1 fresh guanabana leaf

RITUAL

AFTER A WARM SHOWER OR BATH, WEAR YOUR MOST COZY PAJAMAS. DIM THE LIGHTS AND LIGHT A FEW WHITE CANDLES TO CREATE A SERENE SETTING WHILE YOU CALMLY PREPARE THE POTION.

METHOD

★ Crush the guanabana leaves using a mortar and pestle, add them to a serving mug and pour in the hot water.

★ Allow the herbal infusion to steep for a minimum of 3 mins (or microwave for 1 min).

★ Remove the leaves and discard them, thanking them for their help.

★ Stir in the citrus juice and sweetener to taste. Garnish with a slice of lemon and a fresh guanabana leaf, and enjoy!

THE WITCHES PYRAMID

The Witches Pyramid is a philosophy of thought meant to demonstrate the foundation of magickal arts. It represents the four cornerstones of understanding needed to excel in Witchcraft with the pinnacle or top point representing our balanced understanding of the former four. The name comes from the fact that this philosophy is usually symbolized through the image of a pyramid. I will explain the Witches Pyramid in the context of this book.

TO KNOW
Element: Air
True knowledge comes from experience.

To understand and do research on which herbs, crystals or other ingredients may be poisonous. The listed recipes in this book are safe to ingest but if you intend on creating your own brews, ointments, elixirs, tonics, tinctures or washes, educate yourself with due diligence on what is safe to come into contact with the human body as well as our plant and animal friends.

TO DARE
Element: Water
Practice makes perfect.

Becoming a master at a skill does not happen overnight. It takes an incredible amount of perseverance, courage and daring to keep getting back up after you fall. Failure is just another opportunity to learn a different strategy to get it right. To dare also refers to having the strength to look yourself in the eye and not bullshit yourself. To have the power to work on bettering yourself and your life is an achievement in anyone's book.

TO WILL
Element: Fire
Is your heart in it?

It takes great willpower to harness our rambunctious mind to focus on the task at hand. That willingness to focus your thoughts and practice visualization, and the ability to continue reaching for these goals with good ol'-fashioned hard work, is the difference between living the life of your dreams or settling on a dead-end job. What are you made of? You need to light a fire under that ass and get to work on achieving the things you want in life.

TO BE SILENT
Element: Earth
Silence can speak volumes.

There is something to be said for people who know how to keep a secret. They are the ones that can create blueprints of their future and work step-by-step to achieving it without letting a soul know what they're up to until they get there. Suddenly everyone turns to see their success and wonders how they managed to build that wonderful life. The reason they accomplished such greatness is because they did not need to hire a hundred different architects to design their perfect vision.

TO GO
Element: Spirit
What's inside counts.

True fulfilment comes from balancing all of the other cornerstones within yourself. It means applying the knowledge you've gained from life's experiences, refusing to stay down when life hands you obstacles, going after your greatest passions in life and not giving a damn what anyone else thinks or says about it.

healing

HEALING

POTIONS

HEALING
POTIONS

Health is one of – if not the most – prized aspect of our lives. The reason for this is directly tied to the fact that the state of our health gives us insight into the timing of our lifeline. Making health a major priority ensures you are able to live life to the fullest and that it is a long and happy one.

Today, there are healthy choices at most restaurants and fast-food vendors. Our supermarkets have bountiful supplies of fresh produce and sometimes even green smoothie stations. It seems that health is within arm's reach, if only we could choose it over decadence. Overindulging in gluttonous foods is just as detrimental as indulging in harmful behaviors. Both are unhealthy lifestyle choices for your body and mind.

For all those who have been looking for a sign to cleanse themselves of noxious relationships that are disadvantageous to their growth, or to cut the cords of an eating behavior that is a health risk, this is your sign. Return to a more natural and lively state by setting an intention for a fresh start. These potions were created and crafted to assist in new beginnings, to prevent ailments from befalling you and to restore your vitality.

Note: These potions are not medical in purpose. If you need medical attention, please seek out a health professional. Research each ingredient before attempting to take it internally in any fashion. These are for magickal association and purposes only.

For vegan substitutes please see page 28.

CORRESPONDENCES

INCENSE

carnation, eucalyptus, frankincense, gardenia, myrrh, rosemary, sandalwood

CRYSTALS TO WORK WITH FOR HEALING SPELLS

green agate, fuchsite, jade, green jasper, red jasper, jet, larimar, peridot, staurolite, pink topaz

DAYS OF THE WEEK FOR HEALING SPELLS

Monday, Sunday

PLANETS FOR HEALING SPELLS

Moon, Sun

ZODIAC SIGNS FOR HEALING SPELLS

Leo, Aries, Sagittarius

MOON PHASES FOR HEALING SPELLS

Waning Moon

FIRST AID KIT

This is the perfect elixir to drink before you travel, to prevent an oncoming illness after sitting in a vacuum-sealed airplane in close quarters for hours on end with others who may be ill. You can thank the Goddess for strengthening your immune system through the power of this impactful potion. Every ingredient within this elixir is associated with healing and ensuring your health is in tip-top shape, so be sure to drink every last drop if you're feeling a sniffle coming on.

Key correspondences included in this drink are:

ORANGE. Also known as the fruit of joy, this lively fruit has the power to awaken your senses with its very scent. Oranges are associated with love magick, fertility, a magickal boost for spells, divination, success, prosperity, strengthening relationships and health and wellness.

ANISE HYSSOP. Hyssop is a member of the mint family and has the ability to soothe symptoms like sore and irritated throats. Hyssop has been used for centuries to help heal injuries and ailments.

LEMON BALM. Lemon Balm is used in spells to bring animal healing, compassion, endings, fertility, happiness, healing, longevity, love, mental healing, prosperity, psychic enhancement, release, success and youth.

INGREDIENTS

★ Juice of 3 oranges
★ 5 tbsp anise hyssop simple syrup (see below)
★ 1 anise hyssop tea bag (or 1 tbsp dried anise hyssop)
★ ½ teaspoon dried lemon balm

For the anise hyssop simple syrup:
★ 200g/7oz/ 1 cup caster/ granulated sugar
★ 240ml/8fl oz/ 1 cup water

Magickal Garnish
★ Hyssop flower buds
★ ½ orange slice

RITUAL

DRINK THIS FACING AN EASTWARD WINDOW DURING THE DAY AND IMAGINE THE SUN'S RAYS FILLING UP YOUR ENTIRE BEING TO CLEANSE YOU OF ANY TOXINS.

METHOD

★ Make the syrup by putting the sugar and water into a saucepan over a medium heat, stirring until the sugar dissolves. Bring to the boil, add in the anise hyssop and dried lemon balm, then turn off the heat. Allow to steep for 1 hour, then strain. Can be stored in a glass jar in the refrigerator for up to a week.

★ Make the drink by mixing together the orange juice with the anise hyssop simple syrup in a serving glass.

★ Garnish with hyssop flower buds and half an orange slice, and enjoy.

TRANQUILI-TEA

We could all use a little help easing our daily worries and anxieties, removing the palm glued to our forehead and just giving ourselves a much-needed break. Think of this potion as a soothing friend offering a shoulder to cry on, a word of wisdom and a warm hug. This is the perfect drink to get you back on your feet for those days when you just can't even.

Key correspondences included in this drink are:

PEPPERMINT. Peppermint has long been used in healing potions and mixtures. Peppermint also has a long history in purification spells. The fresh leaves rubbed against the head are said to relieve headaches. Peppermint worn at the wrist assures that you will not get ill. Its presence raises the vibrations of an area.

CHAMOMILE. This little white and yellow flower is associated with spells for money, peace, love, tranquility and purification.

VALERIAN. This plant is associated with love, calm and sleep, and allows those that are in dispute to reconnect and come together.

INGREDIENTS

★ 225ml/7½fl oz/ 1 cup hot water

★ ¼ tsp each of dried valerian, chamomile and peppermint (or a tea bag containing them)

★ Sweetener of your choice, to taste

RITUAL

AFTER TAKING A WARM, SOOTHING SHOWER WHERE YOU IMAGINE YOUR TROUBLES WASHING DOWN THE DRAIN, PUT ON YOUR MOST COMFORTABLE PAJAMAS. BREW THE POTION AND DRINK IT WHILE WATCHING A COMEDY OR LISTENING TO SOOTHING MUSIC. THEN GO TAKE A NAP, SWEETIE, YOU'LL FEEL BETTER WHEN YOU WAKE UP.

METHOD

★ In the hot water, steep your valerian, chamomile and peppermint for 3 mins.

★ Strain, and pour herbal infusion into a cozy mug and sweeten to taste.

★ Enjoy!

SILVER LINING

Trust in the power of black sesame and green tea to bring a positive outlook in darker times. This potion will rebalance your stormy mood and lighten whatever weighs heavy on your mind. Drink this routinely each morning if the emotional forecast calls for stormy weather.

Key correspondences included in this drink are:

GREEN TEA. Matcha is made from powdered green tea leaves. Green tea is associated with luck, health, love, passion, energy, cleansing and money-drawing spells.

SESAME. Sesame has the power to open doors, create new opportunities, invite new perspectives, instill hope and dispel depression and negativity.

HEMPSEED MILK. Hemp is associated with positive energy, manifestation, healing, protection, peace, meditation, removal of negative influences, love, binding and psychic visions.

INGREDIENTS

- ★ 175ml/6fl oz/ ¾ cup steamed hempseed milk (coconut milk is a great alternative)
- ★ 1 tsp matcha powder
- ★ 2 tbsp Torani candied sesame syrup (or 1 tbsp tahini + 1 tbsp syrup sweetener), plus extra to serve
- ★ 3½ tbsp boiling water

Magickal Garnish
- ★ Top with sesame seeds arranged in a happy face

RITUAL

TURN ON ALL LIGHTS, BRIGHTENING YOUR SPACE AS MUCH AS POSSIBLE. PLACE A CLEAR QUARTZ ON YOUR PERSON (IN YOUR POCKET, HAND, ETC.). ALLOW THE CRYSTAL TO ABSORB ANY NEGATIVE ENERGIES. PLACE IT IN SUNLIGHT AFTER TO CLEANSE.

METHOD

★ Whisk together the steamed milk, matcha, sesame syrup and boiling water in a jug.

★ Pour this hot tea into a serving mug and add additional syrup to taste. Garnish with the sesame seeds.

★ Enjoy, and keep your chin up, love!

APPLE OF MY EYE

When you apple-solutely need a pick-me-up, this potion has got your back! This legendary fruit will bring you a surge of positive power and tons of health benefits. After all, an apple a day keeps the doctor away.

Key correspondences included in this drink are:

ALLSPICE. Allspice is very uplifting and has the power to increase energy, determination and luck.

APPLE. Apples are known for their healing properties and ability to assist in all health and love magick.

CIDER. Cider is made from the fermented juice of apples and is considered a positive force to be reckoned with.

CLOVE. Cloves are used to attract good luck and prosperity, keep friends close and stop malicious gossip.

HONEY. Like other sweeteners, honey has long been associated with a deep, resonating connection, enduring health, love and prosperity.

CINNAMON. Cinnamon has long been associated with feelings of coziness, strength, empowerment and safety. It's also widely used in workings for healing, home protection, love and lust spells, money drawing, quickening spells and to draw success and victory to you.

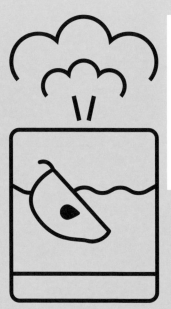

INGREDIENTS

★ 125ml/4fl oz/
½ cup pressed
apple juice
(fresh is best,
but use what
you've got!)
★ 125ml/4fl oz/
½ cup strong/
hard cider
★ 2 cloves

★ 2 whole
allspice berries
★ 2 sticks of
cinnamon
★ 2 tbsp honey
or other
sweetener of
your choice,
plus extra
to serve

RITUAL

LIGHT A GREEN
CANDLE WHILE
PREPARING THIS
POTION AND
VISUALIZE, AS IT
BURNS DOWN, THAT
IT IS BURNING AWAY
ANY PHYSICAL,
MENTAL OR
SPIRITUAL AILMENTS
YOU HAVE.

METHOD

★ In a cleansed cooking pot over a low
heat, brew all the ingredients together for
at least 30 mins on a low simmer.

★ Add additional sweetener to taste.

★ Strain into a serving mug and enjoy!

FTW

Sometimes you need a champion on your side to win whatever battles face you. Allow me to introduce you to your hero: the tomato. This powerful fruit is filled with the antioxidant lycopene, vitamin C, potassium, folate and vitamin K. Add in some serious kick with cayenne, black pepper and ground ginger and you have a fiery conqueror ready for battle. This is the perfect potion for those looking for something on the savory side and will definitely bring some color to your cheeks.

Key correspondences included in this drink are:

TOMATO. Tomatoes are associated with keeping depression away. They contain folic acid, which prevents the excess formation of homocysteine, which when overproduced can block our happy hormones. Tomatoes are associated with love, money, prosperity and healing magick.

BLACK PEPPER AND CAYENNE PEPPER. These peppers are associated with banishing, binding, creating confusion, dispelling curses, exorcism, protection from evil, stopping gossip and warding off jealousy.

POMEGRANATE. Pomegranate juice has long been used in health magick due to its blood-like color. It is filled with antioxidants, such as vitamin C.

INGREDIENTS

- ★ 1 tsp sea salt
- ★ ¼ tsp cayenne pepper
- ★ ¼ tsp ground ginger
- ★ ¼ tsp ground black pepper
- ★ Ice cubes
- ★ 2 tbsp vodka (optional)

- ★ 125ml/4fl oz/ ½ cup tomato vegetable juice (such as V8)
- ★ 3½ tbsp pomegranate juice

Magickal Garnish
- ★ Stuffed olives

RITUAL

ONCE YOU DOWN THE POTION, POUND YOUR CHEST WITH YOUR RIGHT FIST THREE TIMES, SAYING: "I CALL UPON THE POWER OF ARES! CONQUER ALL MY ADVERSARIES!" WHILE IMAGINING THE GREEK GOD SLASHING DOWN WHATEVER AILS YOU.

METHOD

- ★ Mix together the sea salt, cayenne pepper, ground ginger and black pepper. Wet the rim of a tall serving glass with water, then dip it into the spice mixture.

- ★ Fill the glass with ice.

- ★ Mix all the remaining ingredients together and pour into the prepared serving glass.

- ★ Garnish with stuffed olives and enjoy.

Protection

PROTECTION

POTIONS

PROTECTION POTIONS

We all have a need to feel safe in our home, school, workplace or really everywhere we travel! Those who have ever experienced a breach or loss of security in their most sacred spaces will know that once it's lost it can be very challenging to reclaim. This is why through the art of potion-making we'll be working to instill a sense of safety and security throughout our favorite spaces, within ourselves and in our digital life.

When it comes to protection from a Witch's perspective, one common practice usually comes to mind: protection magick. Protection magick is either defensive or offensive. A commonly used defensive magickal practice is the creation of wards, for example, casting a protective circle around yourself or magickal space. Other types of wards include talismans, charms or amulets. Offensive magickal practices deal with banishing, binding or reversal magick. We'll be utilizing a bit of both in these potions.

We all deserve to live our lives as we see fit without suffering from a primal fear of being unsafe. It's our right to live loud, proud and wild for as long as we please (respectful of noise ordinances, of course!). We have the right to be our truest selves in our private spaces and feel comfortable being who we are, wherever we go.

Sanctuary is only a sip away! Through use of the following correspondences we'll begin safeguarding and setting up magickal sentries to bring you the peace of mind you deserve.

For vegan substitutes please see page 28.

CORRESPONDENCES

INCENSE

bay, cedar, clove, dragon's blood, frankincense and myrrh, pepper, rosemary, sage, sandalwood, valerian, wormwood, yerba santa

CRYSTALS TO WORK WITH FOR PROTECTION SPELLS

agate, alum, amber, amethyst, angelite, apache tears, aquamarine, aventurine, carnelian, cat's eye, citrine, lepidolite, lodestone, snowflake obsidian, onyx, black tourmaline, tanzanite, tiger's eye

DAYS OF THE WEEK FOR PROTECTION SPELLS

Tuesday, Saturday, Sunday

PLANETS FOR PROTECTION SPELLS

Mars, Saturn, Sun

ZODIAC SIGNS FOR PROTECTION SPELLS

Aries, Scorpio, Capricorn

MOON PHASE FOR PROTECTION SPELLS

Full Moon

SAFE & SOUND

Using the power of sound and resonance, we'll imbue your space and potion with protection. As a lover of all things boba, I wanted to include as many magickal boba drinks as possible! This potion is brimming with the protective powers of black tea, cinnamon, clove and salt. For an added boost of protection, use the milk recommendations below.

Key correspondences included in this drink are:

BLACK TEA. Black tea is created from fermented tea leaves and is associated with banishing lower energies, bringing about feelings of encouragement and stimulating your mind into action (due to the caffeine).

CINNAMON. Cinnamon has long been associated with feelings of coziness, strength, empowerment and safety. It's also widely used in workings for healing, home protection, love and lust spells, money drawing, quickening spells and to draw success and victory to you.

CLOVES. Cloves are used in magick to attract good luck, prosperity, keep good friends close and stop malicious gossip.

NON-DAIRY MILKS. Soy milk, coconut milk, hemp milk, rice milk and flaxseed milk are all associated with protection.

INGREDIENTS

- 40g/1½oz/ ¼ cup tapioca pearls/boba balls
- 200g/7oz/ 1 cup dark brown sugar
- Pinch of ground cinnamon
- Pinch of ground cloves
- 1 black tea bag
- 240ml/8fl oz/ 1 cup cold milk
- 230ml/8fl oz/ scant 1 cup boiling water
- Squirty cream
- Pinch of sea salt

Magickal Garnish
- Black lava sea salt (or regular sea salt)
- Extra syrup for pentacle symbol

RITUAL

DRAWING A PENTACLE WITH BOBA SYRUP ON TOP OF POTION, SING, "GUARDIANS AND LOVING ENERGIES THAT BE, I DRAW UPON YOUR POWER AND CALL OUT TO THEE! EMPOWER THIS POTION ENCIRCLED IN SALT, AND MAKE MY SPACE SAFE LIKE A LOVING VAULT!"

METHOD

★ Prepare your serving glass by wetting the rim with water and then dipping it in black lava sea salt (or regular salt).

★ Prepare your tapioca pearls/boba balls following the packet instructions. In a bowl, mix the cooked, strained tapioca pearls/ boba balls with the sugar, the cinnamon and ground cloves, creating a syrupy mixture of sweetened boba.

★ With a spoon, collect some syrup from the boba and draw a pentacle on the inside of the glass, imbuing it with protection.

★ In another mug, steep the tea bags in the water for 3 mins, then discard the tea bags. Allow to cool for about 3–5 mins.

★ Put 3 tbsp of the boba syrup in the serving glass and swirl to coat the glass.

★ Add the brewed tea and milk, leaving room for the cream. Top with the squirty cream and sprinkle on the sea salt.

CYBER SECURITY

Let's face it, the majority of our life is lived online and with this lifestyle choice comes risky territory (not risqué territory, please see the love potions chapter for more on that!).

This brew is perfect to protect you from embarrassing digital faux pas, creating proper boundaries for those trying to invade your online personal space, and it shoos away pesky passive aggressive comments that were only sent to put you down. Our online life deserves cleansing and protecting as much as the other areas of our life. This potion provides the online protection you've been looking for.

Key correspondences included in this drink are:

RED CHILLI. Red chillies have a long history of "hot footing" works of magick to banish people from your life but are also commonly used as a way to spice up any romantic relationship. Chillies should be handled with care. Be sure to wash your hands thoroughly after slicing chillies and avoid contact with your eyes and other sensitive areas.

PINEAPPLE. Associated with good luck, prosperity, strengthening self-esteem and willpower, attracting quality hospitality, expressing warmth to others, welcoming strangers and viewing others as friends.

MANGO. Mangoes are a magickal fruit that are most commonly used in workings to encourage fond feelings, inspire love or a budding romance.

INGREDIENTS

★ 1 spicy red chilli
★ 4 tbsp rum
★ 2 tbsp mango purée
★ Ice cubes

★ 175ml/6fl oz/ ¾ cup pineapple juice

Magickal Garnish
★ Red chilli slices

RITUAL

OPEN YOUR WINDOW CURTAINS TO ALLOW SUNLIGHT TO SHINE ON TO YOUR DIGITAL DEVICE, WHICH REPRESENTS THE WINDOW OR PORTAL TO YOUR ONLINE LIFE. IMAGINE THE SUNLIGHT CLEANSING THE TOXICITY EXPERIENCED THERE AND REPLACING IT WITH WARMTH AND HAPPINESS.

METHOD

★ Slice the chilli into thin rings and then put them into a cocktail shaker.

★ Add the rum, mango purée and a handful of ice and shake vigorously for 30 secs.

★ Add the pineapple juice and continue shaking for an additional 30 secs.

★ Pour the potion into a tall serving glass filled with ice and garnish with more chilli slices. Enjoy!

FIREWALL

Personal boundaries are invisible spaces around us that reinforce our comfort, safety and security. When others in our immediate environment neglect the importance of our personal boundaries, whether intentionally or not, it's our duty to reinforce them.

This fiery red potion has the force you need to keep those personal-space intruders far, far away from you. It's ideal for those moments of tension between classmates, co-workers, neighbors or others you share a communal space with because this potion will burn away the tension with the power of fire, then bring a cool, calming energy to the situation with the power of ice.

Key correspondences included in this drink are:

RED CHILLI. Red chillies have a long history of "hot footing" works of magick to banish people from your life but are also commonly used as a way to spice up any romantic relationship.

HIBISCUS. Hibiscus has been utilized for a long time as an aphrodisiac to encourage love, lust and passion from others where it was not present. It is also used in workings of divination to enhance psychic abilities and prophetic dreams.

LEMON. This citrus helps remove unwanted energies that may be blocking your path to success. It is used to cleanse, provide spiritual openings, purify and remove all blockages.

INGREDIENTS

★ 100ml/3½fl oz/
scant ½ cup
hibiscus syrup
(see right)

★ 2 tbsp lemon
juice

★ 3½ tbsp vodka
or gin

★ 1 whole red chilli
(use less if you
are sensitive
to spice)

★ Ice cubes

**For the
hibiscus syrup:**

★ 125ml/4fl oz/
generous ½ cup
honey or other
sweetener

★ 240ml/8fl oz/
1 cup water

★ 1 tbsp dried
hibiscus flowers

Magickal Garnish

★ Lime slices
★ Mint sprigs
★ Sliced red
chillies

RITUAL

MENTALLY CALL
UPON THE POWER
OF FIRE AND ICE
TO BREAK THE
EMOTIONAL CORD
THAT FEEDS THE
CONNECTION
BETWEEN YOU
AND THE OTHER
INDIVIDUAL(S),
WHILE ALSO
SOOTHING THE
SEPARATION TO
ALLOW FOR A
NEW BEGINNING.

METHOD

★ To make the hibiscus syrup, put the
honey and water into a saucepan over a
medium heat and bring to the boil. Add the
dried hibiscus and stir until the honey is
fully dissolved. Remove from the heat and
let steep for 13 mins, then cool completely
for 30 mins. Strain through a sieve/fine
mesh strainer into a sealed jar or other
glass container. This can be stored in the
refrigerator for up to 2 weeks.

★ To create the potion, put all the
ingredients for the magickal brew into a
cocktail shaker with some ice and shake
vigorously for 30 secs.

★ Strain into a short serving glass filled
with ice, and garnish with lime slices, fresh
mint sprigs and sliced red chillies.

MELON WARDS

When's the last time you asked yourself how you're feeling, and actually listened? Checking in on your emotional state is important to maintaining mental health. And our emotions need protection just as much as anything else in our life. If you feel you've been neglecting your emotional health and wish to do some inner healing and protection work, then a sip from this potion will do just the trick.

Create a protection ward by facing each direction and asking the associated element to protect yourself and your space. Start facing East and finish facing North. (East = Air, South = Fire, West = Water, North = Earth). You can say something as simple as, "Energies of the East, I call out to you. Send protection to my sacred space, imbued."

Key correspondence included in this drink:

HONEYDEW MELON. (Can be substituted for wintermelon or watermelon.) Honeydew melons and melons in general are associated with fertility, beauty, youth, longevity and abundance. They have the power to generate love and happiness in relationships and can promote self-love. Melons can help in clearing energy blockages, unburdening your heart and releasing old pain.

INGREDIENTS

★ 150g/5oz/
1 cup chopped
honeydew
melon flesh

★ 2 scoops of
vanilla ice cream

★ 2 tbsp Amoretti
honeydew
melon syrup

★ 70g/2½oz/
½ cup ice cubes

Magickal Garnish

★ Slices of melon
in the shape of
a heart

RITUAL

WHETHER IT'S FOR
1 HOUR OR AN
ENTIRE WEEKEND,
DEDICATE SOME
TIME FOR SELF-
LOVE AND HEALING.
DURING THIS TIME,
DO WHAT MAKES
YOU THE MOST
HAPPY WHILE
YOU IMBIBE THIS
MELONY POTION.

METHOD

★ Put all the ingredients into a blender
and blend until smooth. This will take about
30 secs.

★ Pour the potion into a serving glass.
Garnish with heart-shaped melon slices,
and enjoy!

FUN IS THE MAIN INGREDIENT IN WITCHCRAFT

I want you to play a little game with me. Yes, right this minute you and I will have a bit of fun. I want you to imagine you are six years old again. Now imagine you've just woken up in your most favorite pajamas and it's Saturday morning. You feel alive and full of energy while you zip downstairs, skipping the last few steps as you land with a giggle. Then you sprint full speed into the kitchen to find your favorite breakfast waiting for you. You gobble up your breakfast, take a bubble bath and prepare for the day. Now tell me, what would you like to do? "Have fun!" you shout in reply! So fun is exactly what's on the agenda.

Shall we play pretend? All right then, let's pretend we live in a magickal world full of enchantment where people have powers and

magickal abilities. Imagine that whatever your heart desires can be yours as long as you wish for it clearly and let the magick take it from there. You start wishing for a peanut butter and jelly sandwich with a tall glass of milk and a fun new video game to play. Over the next hour or so, whoever you run into in your house, you tell them about your PB&J wish and desire for a new video game. By lunchtime, a surprise is waiting for you on a plate in the kitchen... your dream sandwich has arrived! And after that, there's shopping with mum and you get to stop by the game store afterwards for a new game. Life couldn't get better than this, you think pleasantly. Wishes really do come true.

Was that game of pretend fun? Did you know that magick works exactly as described in our little story? Six-year-old you wasn't concerned about how the PB&J or new game would find its way to you, only that you'd be even more happy if you got it! Magick found the path of least resistance to deliver it right away. The same can be said with every other spell. Focus more on the joy of imagining the goal; try to use all your senses to really feel its presence in your life, or maybe even do activities that will bring the result to you even faster.

Let's take, for example, a love spell. Six-year old you is now twenty-three, and looking for L – O – V – E. The only problem is you never leave the house, self-care is the lowest thing on your priority list and, oh yeah, you want the other person to be absolutely perfect and somehow find their way to your doorstep all by themselves. An idea comes to you: "What if I showed myself some love, affection and attention. Then head out for an afternoon walking around town to find a new café?" And so you do, and you find a great café. The first time you go you don't find that special someone, but the barista is pretty cool. By the fifth time, you're a regular and the barista is looking rather cute today. Add a little flirtation, common goals and genuine friendship and we've got ourselves a winner! Sure, it didn't happen with a snap of your fingers, but with a little effort and magick to spark some inspiration, you did reach your end goal.

transformation

TRANSFORMATION

POTIONS

TRANSFORMATION POTIONS

One of the most amazing things about magick is it can help you transform into the person you've always wanted to become. A common misconception about magick is that results happen instantly and with almost little to no effort on the caster's part. While I'm not here to burst your magick bubble I do want to provide clarity on this misconception. Magick most certainly has the capability to create an impactful change in your life, but it will do so over time.

Whether you want to transform your love life, your attractiveness, your job or how your classmates treat you, these potions will directly alter your current circumstances to align with your goal. The most important ingredient when it comes to transformation spells, as with any magickal working, is intention. If your willpower is strong and you couple any magickal working with hard work in the mundane world as well, you'll see those changes happen even quicker.

It should be noted that there are no spells or magickal workings that can transform a human, no matter their magickal prowess, into a mermaid, dragon, fae creature, vampire or werewolf. DNA cannot be manipulated by magick and I don't want to waste anyone's time with fantasy. There's a time and place for that at the *Dungeons & Dragons* table, where I always have a seat as a half-elf wizard. This book contains legitimate magickal potions and instructions to create real change in your life.

The following potions provide an effective change in yourself or surroundings, transmute your capabilities and draw out your inner power.

For vegan substitutes please see page 28.

CORRESPONDENCES

INCENSE
almond, camphor, clary sage, rose, white poppy, passionflower

PLANET FOR TRANSFORMATION SPELLS
Moon

CRYSTALS TO WORK WITH FOR TRANSFORMATION SPELLS
amber, cat's eye, moonstone, pearl, silver

ZODIAC SIGNS FOR TRANSFORMATION SPELLS
Gemini, Leo, Scorpio

DAY OF THE WEEK FOR TRANSFORMATION SPELLS
Monday

MOON PHASES FOR TRANSFORMATION SPELLS
New Moon

CHRYSALIS

For those pivotal moments when you need to change direction, this potion will transform you. The truly remarkable part of the Chrysalis is the ritual: a glamour spell. Glamours are an ancient form of illusion magick that allow others to view us the way we wish to be seen. To attain the glamour, you need to embody a new character you'll create.

Character creation may come naturally to those with a role-playing or acting background, but everyone has the ability to take on the personality of someone else. This chameleon-like behavior is natural and normal; many of us do it daily. For example, when a person watches a new show, anime, K-drama or movie and begins seeing the protagonist as a role model. They begin embodying their traits and characteristics, maybe even dressing and acting like them. This is the power of a glamour, a transformative illusory act. So pretend your life is a video-game character-selection screen and create your character!

Key correspondences included in this drink are:

LIME. Removes unwanted energies that may be blocking your path to success. Used to cleanse, provide spiritual openings and purify.

KIWI. Associated with revealing secrets, looking for answers, happiness, sex and physical longings, and good luck.

BUTTERFLY PEA. When these flowers are brewed they create a deep blue tea that transforms in color when it is mixed with citrus.

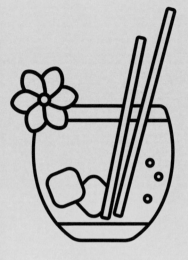

INGREDIENTS

- ★ 2 tbsp kiwi fruit juice (no pulp)
- ★ Crushed ice
- ★ 3 fresh mint leaves, muddled or crushed
- ★ 2 tbsp freshly squeezed lime juice
- ★ 1 tbsp agave or other sweetener of your choice
- ★ 1 tbsp crème de menthe
- ★ 2 tbsp vodka
- ★ 1 tbsp brewed butterfly pea tea

Magickal Garnish
- ★ A few butterfly pea flowers

RITUAL

CREATE A CHARACTER TO EMBODY FOR YOUR GLAMOUR SPELL AND PRACTICE WEARING THIS CHARACTER WHILE YOUR BUTTERFLY PEA TEA BREWS. REMEMBER THAT THE POWER OF A GLAMOUR SPELL LASTS AS LONG AS YOU CAN MAINTAIN THE CHARACTER.

METHOD

★ Add the kiwi fruit juice to a short serving glass filled with crushed ice.

★ Put the mint, lime juice and sweetener into a bowl and muddle (mix and stir) until the mint leaves are crushed. Add the mint mixture to your serving glass.

★ Add the crème de menthe.

★ Add the shot of vodka and top with the butterfly pea tea. Garnish with butterfly pea flowers.

★ Enjoy as a layered drink, or stir well.

SHIFTER

We all have a secret side to us that we might only reveal to our most trusted, coveted friends. For those moments when you either want to suppress a certain troublesome characteristic for a few hours, or alternatively if you wish to fully unleash the truth of who you are, then this potion will allow you to do so. Be it beast or buddy, the power always lies within you to decide.

You will need an ice cube tray and a black light to enjoy this potion at its best.

Key correspondence included in this drink:

MINT. This herb is known to draw customers to a business and promote financial success. The dried leaves are used in luck and prosperity spells to bring wealth to the caster. In Greek mythology, the maiden Minthe was dazzled by Hades and made an attempt to seduce him, but Queen Persephone intervened and metamorphosed Minthe into the common garden variety of mint.

INGREDIENTS

- ★ Tonic water
- ★ 2 tbsp vanilla vodka (or regular vodka)
- ★ 2 tbsp peppermint schnapps
- ★ 125ml/4fl oz/ ½ cup lemon-lime soda
- ★ 3 fresh mint leaves

Magickal Garnish
- ★ Peppermint candy

RITUAL

BURN DRAGON'S BLOOD INCENSE TO ASSIST IN THE SHIFT YOU'D LIKE TO SEE. WHILE BREWING THIS POTION, FOCUS ON WHICH SPECIFIC CHARACTERISTICS YOU'D EITHER LIKE TO SUBDUE OR BRING OUT WITHIN YOURSELF.

METHOD

★ Prepare tonic water ice cubes by filling an ice cube tray with tonic water. Freeze until solid.

★ Crush your peppermint candy in a shallow dish. Line the rim of a tall serving glass by first dipping it in water and then into the crushed candy.

★ Fill your serving glass with tonic water ice cubes. Pour in the vodka and schnapps.

★ Top with the lemon-lime soda and add the mint leaves.

★ Turn off the lights and turn on your black light to reveal the shifter within this potion.

REVAMP

This dual-toned potion has the dark power of cocoa with a sensual boldness from the red velvet cream top. It is the perfect concoction to suffuse you with allure and entice anyone that crosses your path. Drink the potion and then follow-up with the ritual, and your enchantment will be complete.

Key correspondences included in this drink are:

CINNAMON. Cinnamon is one of the most excellent correspondences for transformation magick as it both heats up love situations and invites spicy romances to ensue.

CHOCOLATE. This potion contains chocolate in the form of Dutch-process black cocoa powder and red velvet emulsion. Chocolate historically has been used as a precious gift to loved ones and in ancient times had a higher value than gold. Chocolate is associated with love in all forms and is used in magickal workings to gain power.

PRIMROSE. Primrose is a flower deeply connected to the Moon and the feminine aspect within each of us. It helps in communication and building strong relationships with our loved ones. Dried primrose buds and petals can be found online on sites like Amazon. Alternatively, you can find dried rose buds and petals online as well.

INGREDIENTS

- ★ 125ml/4fl oz/ ½ cup coconut milk (or other milk alternative)
- ★ 2 tbsp cinnamon sugar (see p. 40)
- ★ 1 tbsp Dutch-process black cocoa powder (or any very dark cocoa powder)

- ★ 3½ tbsp whole milk/half and half
- ★ 2 tbsp sweet beet syrup (or 1 tbsp cherry syrup as an alternative)

Magickal Garnish
- ★ Primrose flowers

RITUAL

HOLDING THREE PRIMROSE BUDS, LET ATTRACTION, SEDUCTION AND ALLURE INFUSE YOU. IMAGINE HEADS TURNING AS YOU WALK INTO A ROOM, PLACING EVERYONE UNDER YOUR THRALL. WHISPER: "ONE TO MAKE THEM GLANCE THIS WAY, TWO TO MAKE THEM WANT TO STAY AND THREE TO MAKE IT LAST ALL DAY."

METHOD

★ In a saucepan, warm the coconut milk over a low heat until simmering, then take off the heat and whisk in the cinnamon sugar and cocoa powder. Pour the hot mixture into a serving mug.

★ In a bowl, whisk together the whole milk/half and half and the sweet beet syrup/cherry syrup until combined, then add this to the serving mug.

★ Garnish with primrose flowers and enjoy!

happy home

HAPPY HOME

POTIONS

HAPPY HOME POTIONS

Your home is your sacred space, which should reflect and celebrate who you are. All the magick that you work within this sacred space will vary in success depending on how well-kept your space is, how energetically clean it is and what type of decoration it's adorned with. This is because your home is an extension of you, and the other people you live with. It collects and is steeped in our energies, so it's important to be mindful of how you feel there on a regular basis and to always be working to create a space that sparks joy (thanks, Marie Kondo).

Creating a happy home does take some effort, but it is absolutely attainable. The best route to take to start seeing a positive shift occur in your home is by starting small. Start with your bedroom, and simply change the sheets and make your bed. Then work on cleaning small areas of your room, like your desk, closet, your altar (if you have one!), shelving, and so on, until each area of your room has been cleansed and spruced to your liking. While this isn't a chapter on throwing away your clutter and doing your two weeks' worth of laundry, it is important to know that our environment has a direct effect on our wellbeing.

It might be time to stop, take a look around and ask yourself, "Does my space truly reflect who I want to be?"

For vegan substitutes please see page 28.

CORRESPONDENCES

INCENSE

cedar, honeysuckle, jasmine, lavender, rosemary, sage, sandalwood, sweetgrass

CRYSTALS TO WORK WITH FOR HAPPY HOME SPELLS

aquamarine, moonstone, mother-of-pearl, opal, pearl, quartz, sapphire, selenite, silver, iron, black tourmaline, obsidian

DAYS OF THE WEEK FOR HAPPY HOME SPELLS

Monday, Saturday

PLANETS FOR HAPPY HOME SPELLS

Saturn, Moon

ZODIAC SIGNS FOR HAPPY HOME SPELLS

Capricorn, Aquarius

MOON PHASE FOR HAPPY HOME SPELLS

Full Moon

SOLID FOUNDATION

When you have a happy home, you'll have a happy life. If you're looking to create a harmonious environment where all feel safe and comfy, this is the potion for you. It's also ideal to assist in detoxing your home from negativity to improve your home's stability and positive energy.

Key correspondences included in this drink are:

LAVENDER. The scent of lavender allegedly attracts sexual interest, enhances your beauty, banishes harmful energies, promotes happiness, increases intelligence and promotes purification.

LEMON VERBENA AND LEMONGRASS. These herbs are used as primary ingredients for magickal workings related to overcoming addiction, breaking bad habits, increasing communication, enhancing divination, eloquence, intelligence and mental faculties. They also assist in self-improvement, study, travel and wisdom.

LEMON. Helps remove unwanted energies that block your path to success. Used to cleanse, provide spiritual openings and purify.

MINT. Mint is known to draw customers to a business and promote financial success. The dried leaves are used in good-luck, success and prosperity spells to bring wealth to the caster.

THYME. This herb has long been associated with workings involving strength and courage. Used to dispel melancholy, hopelessness and other negative energies in order to bring in happiness.

INGREDIENTS

Serves 6

★ 2 tbsp
   lemon juice
★ 500ml/17fl oz/
   2 cups water
★ 240ml/9fl oz/
   1 cup lavender-
   lemon syrup
   (see below)
★ Ice cubes

For the lavender-lemon syrup
★ 200g/7oz/
   1 cup sugar
★ 240ml/9fl oz/
   1 cup water

★ 1 tbsp dried
   culinary
   lavender
★ 2 sprigs fresh
   lavender
★ 3 stalks
   lemongrass
★ 2 tsp loose
   dried lemon
   verbena

Magickal Garnish
★ Mint leaves
★ Lemon slices
★ Fresh lavender
   sprigs
★ Fresh thyme
   sprigs

RITUAL

OPEN ALL
CURTAINS IN THE
AREA TO ALLOW
SUNLIGHT TO FILL
THE SPACE. WRITE
A SMALL NOTE OF
THREE POSITIVE
ATTRIBUTES YOU
SEE IN EACH
PERSON WITHIN
THE HOUSE AND
THEN, AS YOU
POUR A GLASS OF
THIS POTION FOR
THEM, HAND THEM
YOUR SWEET NOTE.

METHOD

★ To make the syrup, place all the syrup
ingredients in a saucepan over a low heat.
Bring the mixture to a simmer and cook for
1 min, whisking until the sugar dissolves.

★ Turn off the heat and allow to cool
completely. Then strain the mixture
through a sieve/fine mesh strainer to
remove the herbs. You can make this in
advance and store in a sealed container in
the refrigerator. It will keep for a week.

★ In a large jug/pitcher, combine the
lemon juice, water and syrup.

★ Pour the mixture into serving glasses
filled with ice. Garnish with mint, lemon
slices and lavender and thyme sprigs.

SAVORY SURVEILLANCE

Share this protective cocktail with friends and family (of drinking age!) to imbue your space and loved ones with protective energies. Nothing says safety and security like an enchanted dirty spice-rimmed martini!

Key correspondences included in this drink are:

SEA SALT. Salt is one of the most powerful magickal ingredients that is widely used across all cultures and in religious rites. Salt may be used to create magickal barriers against unwelcome guests. It also serves to absorb negative energy around it and works as a cleanser and protective resource.

GARLIC. Garlic cloves can be used to stuff poppets (magickal effigies in doll form) intended to negate negative energy. Garlic braids are hung over the door to repel thieves and envious people, and garlic also brings good luck. Overall, garlic is used for protection, strength, spell-breaking and invoking passion.

OLIVES. Olive leaves are used to asperge your house after you've cleansed and blessed it. The fruit and leaves are used to bring good luck.

BAY. Bay laurel leaves have been known to enhance workings involving health and healing. Bay is also associated with protection, psychic enhancement and success with witchcraft.

BASIL. Basil leaves are associated with astral projection, business protection, happiness, love spells, marriage charms, money spells, peace, protection, purification and safe travels.

DILL SEED. Dill is associated with attracting romance, dispelling bad dreams, dispelling jealousy, increasing emotional balance and bringing good luck, love and romance. Dill is also used in protection magick and to bring mental balance.

SAGE. Sage is such a powerful herb and is associated with purification and cleansing. It is used to promote wisdom, bring good luck, build emotional strength and heal grief.

ANISE. Anise pods are used in magickal workings to bring calm energy to a space and promote good luck, protection and psychic awareness.

BLACK PEPPERCORNS. Black pepper is typically used for protection, for use in "hot footing" works of magick to banish people from your life, defensive magick, power and courage.

CLOVES. Cloves are used in magick to attract good luck, prosperity, keep good friends and family close to you and push away malicious gossip.

INGREDIENTS

- ★ Olive oil
- ★ Ice cubes
- ★ 2 tbsp olive brine
- ★ 3½ tbsp dry vermouth
- ★ 3½ tbsp gin or vodka

For the savory salt spice mix:
- ★ ½ tsp sea salt
- ★ ¼ tsp garlic powder
- ★ ¼ tsp ground or crushed bay leaves
- ★ ¼ tsp dried basil
- ★ ¼ tsp dill seeds
- ★ ¼ tsp dried sage
- ★ ¼ tsp aniseed/anise seeds or crushed star anise
- ★ ½ tsp black peppercorns
- ★ ¼ tsp fennel seeds
- ★ ¼ tsp ground cloves

Magickal Garnish
- ★ 3 stuffed olives
- ★ Pinch of sea salt

METHOD

★ To make the savory salt spice mix, grind down to a fine powder all the listed herbs and spices using a mortar and pestle.

★ Fill a shallow bowl or plate with the mixture.

★ Chill a martini glass in the fridge or freezer to get it very cold. Or if you are in a hurry, fill the martini glass with ice and water, let it sit for a few mins, then pour out the ice and water.

★ Line or wet the rim of the martini glass with olive oil, then dip into the spice mixture.

★ Into a cocktail shaker filled with ice, pour the olive brine, vermouth, and the gin or vodka. Shake vigorously until very cold, 30 secs or so.

★ Strain into the chilled martini glass. Garnish with the stuffed olives and a pinch of sea salt.

RITUAL

AFTER RIMMING THE DRINKING GLASS WITH THE PROTECTION SPICE MIXTURE, GO OUTDOORS AND SPRINKLE THE REST IN A CLOCKWISE DIRECTION AROUND YOUR HOME. IF YOU LIVE IN AN APARTMENT BUILDING, YOU CAN SPRINKLE THE POWDER ACROSS YOUR THRESHOLD. DRAW A PENTACLE WITH OLIVE OIL ON THE OUTSIDE OF THE GLASS TO SEAL IN THE PROTECTIVE POWERS OF THIS DRINK.

JOY OF LAUGHTER

Laughter is the best medicine to lift your spirits and create a happy, healthy environment. When your home is filled with the joy of laughter, it is a happy home indeed. Even in the cases when it is a home away from home, this will fill your space with positive energy.

Key correspondences included in this drink are:

BUTTERFLY PEA TEA. Sweet pea plants are associated with magickal workings involving beauty, compassion, fidelity, friendship, happiness, interchanges, joy, love, luck, mediation, pleasure, reconciliation and youth.

PAPAYA. Papaya is used for banishing, cleansing, healing, hex breaking, love, protection and regeneration. The additional tapioca pearls/boba balls that garnish this recipe are intended to further signify papaya seeds.

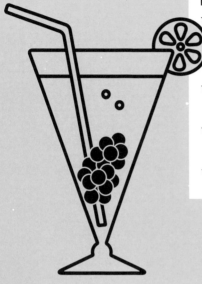

INGREDIENTS **Serves 4**

★ 2 butterfly pea tea bags (or 2 tsp dried butterfly pea flowers)

★ 375ml/13fl oz/ 1½ cups boiling water

★ 125ml/4fl oz/ ½ cup papaya juice

★ 1 tsp vanilla extract

★ 4 tbsp condensed milk

★ 125ml/4fl oz/ ½ cup whole milk/half and half

★ Ice cubes

Magickal Garnish
★ Papaya slices

★ 40g/1½oz/ ¼ cup tapioca pearls/boba balls

RITUAL

PREPARE THIS POTION WITH ANY OF THESE CRYSTALS EITHER ON YOUR PERSON OR NEARBY: AMETHYST, AVENTURINE, BLUE LACE AGATE, EMERALD, JADE, LAPIS LAZULI, SAPPHIRE. PLAY A COMEDIC PODCAST, SHOW OR MOVIE TO GET YOU AND OTHERS AROUND YOU IN A LAUGHING MOOD FOR THE ENTIRETY OF THE POTION-MAKING.

METHOD

★ Create a butterfly pea tea immersion by steeping the tea bags in the boiling water for 3 mins. Remove the tea bags and set the liquid aside to cool.

★ Prepare the tapioca pearls/boba balls (see garnish) according to the packet instructions and set aside to cool, if using.

★ In a bowl, put the papaya juice, condensed milk, whole milk/half and half and vanilla extract and mix to combine.

★ Pour the butterfly pea tea into serving glasses filled halfway with ice, then add the papaya milk mixture.

★ Garnish with papaya slices, and the tapioca pearls/boba balls, if using. Enjoy!

divination

DIVINATION

POTIONS

DIVINATION POTIONS

The ability to attain information from a divine source is the definition of divination. Many of us would love to have the ability to foretell what our grades will be when we graduate, prophesize what our life's mission is or predict the quickest routes to achieving fame and glory. What we're really searching for when it comes to divination are the keys to unlock hidden wisdom just beyond our reach.

There's a reason why the art of fortune-telling was practiced in ancient China, Egypt, Chaldea and Babylonia as far back as 4000 BCE. Humanity has always had a deep-set desire to control the uncontrollable, especially the kingdom-rulers who want to assure the family line is secure. There is nothing more uncontrollable than life, and this is the root of fear for many people. The unpredictability can also be seen as a joyous gift, in that nothing is set in stone and every day is what we make of it. Whether you believe your life has been planned out for you by the hand of destiny or that fate is created through every decision you make, it's clear that the goals are one and the same: joy and happiness for you and your loved ones.

The following recipes will work to aid in predicting your future. They will deliver good fortune and help you rediscover your joys in life.

For vegan substitutes please see page 28.

CORRESPONDENCES

INCENSE

anise, bay, bergamot, cedarwood,
cinnamon, clary sage,
frankincense, sandalwood

CRYSTALS TO WORK WITH
FOR DIVINATION SPELLS

amethyst, bloodstone, lapis lazuli,
obsidian, clear quartz, rose quartz,
sodalite, tiger's eye

DAYS OF THE WEEK FOR
DIVINATION SPELLS

Monday, Wednesday

PLANETS FOR
DIVINATION SPELLS

Mercury, Moon

ZODIAC SIGNS FOR
DIVINATION SPELLS

Virgo, Gemini

MOON PHASES
FOR DIVINATION SPELLS

Dark Moon, Full Moon

CRYSTAL BALL

This potion is perfect for those who'd like to try their hand at the art of crystal ball scrying, all while sipping a delicious cocktail.

Key correspondences included in this drink are:

STAR ANISE. Anise pods are used in magickal workings for clairvoyance, luck, spiritual offerings, protection, power generation, banishing evil, prophetic visions, clarity.
COCONUT MILK. Associated with allure, confidence, diversity, flexibility, protection, psychic awareness, purification, spirituality.

NOTE
*Mugwort extract should not be consumed by those
who are pregnant or breastfeeding.*

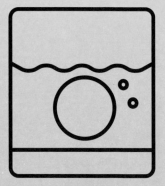

INGREDIENTS

★ 3 star anise pods

★ 175ml/6fl oz/ ¾ cup coconut milk

★ 2 tbsp sweetener

★ 3 tsp Dutch-process black cocoa powder (or any very dark-color cocoa powder)

★ 3 drops mugwort extract

★ ½ tsp instant espresso powder

★ Ice orb (see below)

Magickal Garnish

★ Crystal ice orb for scrying, made from distilled or purified water to create clear ice. Spherical ice tray molds can easily be found online.

RITUAL

THINK OF A QUESTION YOU'D LIKE ANSWERED OR INSIGHT INTO PRIOR TO PREPARING THIS POTION. THEN, AFTER ENSURING YOUR SPACE IS CLEANSED AND PROTECTED, LIGHT A SINGLE CANDLE AND GAZE INTO THE ICE ORB. HOLD THE QUESTION IN YOUR MIND; SEE IF ANY IMAGES, WORDS OR FEELINGS FLASH IN YOUR MIND'S EYE.

METHOD

★ Add the star anise pods to a saucepan with the coconut milk and sweetener, and simmer on a low heat for 5 mins.

★ Turn off heat and remove the pods, then whisk in the black cocoa powder, mugwort extract and espresso powder. Allow the mixture to cool for 5 mins.

★ Pour the cooled black chocolate milk into a tall serving glass and top with an ice orb.

HOROSCOPE POP

It's time to tune into astrology and channel your zodiac sign to create a potion that will enlighten you about your future. The ingredients incorporated in this potion are chosen for their abilities to boost your powers of prophecy. There are four types of Horoscope Pop: the Fiery Salamander for those with Fire signs; the Icey Siren for Water; the Aerie Sylph for Air; and the Rugged Gnome for Earth.

Fire Signs: Aries, Leo, Sagittarius | **Crystals:** carnelian, pyrite, tiger's eye | **Color:** red writing utensil to draw zodiac sign

Water Signs: Cancer, Scorpio, Pisces | **Crystals:** red jasper, citrine, aquamarine | **Color:** blue writing utensil to draw zodiac sign

Air Signs: Gemini, Libra, Aquarius | **Crystals:** labradorite, sodalite, amethyst | **Color:** yellow writing utensil to draw zodiac sign

Earth Signs: Capricorn, Taurus, Virgo | **Crystals:** garnet, petrified wood, moss agate | **Color:** green writing utensil to draw zodiac sign

NOTE

Crystals should be held during potion-making or placed near your working area. Avoid submerging crystals into potions; instead enclose them in tiny sealed glass jars if you intend to perform a crystal submersion or infusion.

RITUAL

USING THE ASSIGNED ELEMENT COLOR, DRAW
YOUR ZODIAC SIGN ON TO A NAPKIN AND PLACE UNDER
YOUR SERVING GLASS WHILE YOU PREPARE YOUR POTION.
ON THE BOTTOM SIDE OF YOUR NAPKIN, WRITE DOWN THE
FUTURE CALENDAR DATE YOU'D LIKE TO LOOK INTO USING
DIVINATION. PLACE YOUR CORRESPONDING CRYSTAL ON
THE NAPKIN AS YOU POUR YOUR POTION.

FIERY SALAMANDER
INGREDIENTS

★ Ice cubes
★ 4 tbsp maraschino cherry syrup
★ 175ml/6fl oz/¾ cup ginger ale
★ 1 cinnamon stick

METHOD

★ To a tall serving glass filled with ice, add
the maraschino cherry syrup.

★ Pour in the ginger ale and add the
cinnamon stick.

★ Stir and enjoy!

ICY SIREN
INGREDIENTS
- ★ 4 tbsp Blue Curaçao liqueur
- ★ Ice cubes
- ★ 175ml/6fl oz/¾ cup lemon-lime soda
- ★ 1 gummy shark

METHOD
★ Add the Curaçao liqueur to a tall serving glass filled with ice.

★ Pour in the lemon-lime soda and add the gummy shark.

★ Stir and enjoy!

AERIE SYLPH
INGREDIENTS
- ★ Ice cubes
- ★ 3½ tbsp pineapple rum
- ★ 175ml/6fl oz/¾ cup pineapple soda
- ★ A scoop of mango sorbet

METHOD
★ To a tall serving glass filled with ice, add the pineapple rum.

★ Pour in the pineapple soda and top with the scoop of mango sorbet. Enjoy!

RUGGED GNOME
INGREDIENTS
★ Ice cubes
★ 3½ tbsp absinthe
★ 125ml/4fl oz/½ cup lemon-lime soda
★ Sprig of fresh mint

METHOD
★ To a tall serving glass filled with ice, add the absinthe.

★ Pour in the lemon-lime soda and finish with a sprig of fresh mint.

★ Stir and enjoy!

THE CARDS SPEAK

This potion allows you to tap into the power of cartomancy, or divination with cards such as tarot. You can simply use everyday playing cards if you don't own a deck of tarot cards. You'll be astounded by the accuracy of what the cards have to say, and what you'll be able to glean from reading into your past, present and future.

Key correspondence included in this drink:

ABSINTHE. An anise-flavored spirit derived from botanicals like wormwood, anise and fennel. Each of these botanicals is associated with drawing love and happiness into your life. The wormwood within absinthe stimulates and enhances psychic abilities.

INGREDIENTS

* 1 tbsp absinthe
* 1 tbsp almond-flavored syrup
* 3½ tbsp double/heavy cream
* 1 egg white (or 2 tbsp pasteurized liquid egg whites)
* Ice cubes

METHOD

★ In a cocktail shaker, combine the absinthe, syrup, cream and egg white.

★ Fill with ice and shake vigorously for at least 30 secs.

★ Strain into a serving glass and enjoy.

RITUAL

SHUFFLE YOUR CARDS, AND DEAL THREE IN A STACK FACE-DOWN UNDER YOUR GLASS. REPEAT THE QUESTION YOU'D LIKE ANSWERED WHILE YOU MAKE YOUR POTION. AS YOU DRINK, TRY TO KEEP YOUR MIND CLEAR, ALLOWING ANY THOUGHTS TO SLIP PAST WITHOUT PONDERING THEM. REMOVE THE CARDS FROM THE GLASS AND TURN THEM OVER, PLACING THEM IN A ROW FROM LEFT TO RIGHT, SO THAT THE CARD THAT WAS ON TOP OF THE PILE IS ON THE LEFT, REPRESENTING YOUR PAST, THE SECOND CARD IS IN THE MIDDLE, REPRESENTING YOUR PRESENT AND THE BOTTOM CARD IS ON THE RIGHT, REPRESENTING YOUR FUTURE. RESEARCH THE MEANINGS OF EACH CARD TO FULLY UNDERSTAND WHAT THE CARDS ARE TELLING YOU.

WHAT TYPE OF WITCH ARE YOU?

Answer the following questions **A**, **B**, **C** or **D** to find out what type of witch you are!

WHAT IS YOUR SUN SIGN?

A Fire sign
(Aries, Leo, Sagittarius)
B Water sign
(Cancer, Scorpio, Pisces)
C Air sign
(Gemini, Libra, Aquarius)
D Earth sign
(Capricorn, Taurus, Virgo)

WHAT IS YOUR IDEAL WEEKEND VACATION?

A A tropical beach, lying in the warm sand under the sun
B Scuba diving exploring a coral reef
C A mountain-top castle getaway with beautiful views
D A cozy cabin in the woods

WHICH OF THE ELEMENTS DO YOU FEEL MOST CONNECTED TO?

A Fire
B Water
C Air
D Earth

WHICH MAGICKAL OBJECT INTRIGUES YOU THE MOST?

A Black-handled blade
B Chalice
C Wand
D Metal pentacle

HOW WOULD YOUR FRIENDS DESCRIBE YOU?

A Wilful and strong-minded! Nothing stands in your way when you go after your goals!

B Introspective and deep. You're always able to know how others are feeling and give them insight on life.

C Fun and free-spirited! You're always ready to do something new and exciting.

D Grounded and wise. You're everyone's go-to advice-giver and always know the right thing to say.

IF YOU COULD HAVE ANY MAGICKAL ABILITY WHICH WOULD YOU CHOOSE?

A Telekinesis

B See auras

C Mind-read

D Control weather

Turn the page to see which type of witch you are...

Mostly As – FIRE WITCH

Fire Witches are drawn to self-empowerment and growing their willpower.

Types of Fire Witch include:

Tech Witch, Draconic Witch, Chaos Witch, Eclectic Witch, Cultural Witch, Sex Witch, Blade Witch, Blood Witch, Vampiric Witch, Wish Witch, Transmutation Witch, Warrior Witch, Demonic Witch, Aphrodisiac Witch, Hereditary Witch, Energy Witch, Enchanter Witch, Secular Witch, Guardian Witch, Evocation Witch, Justice Witch, Lightning Witch, Candle Witch, Hearthfire Witch, Wildfire Witch

Mostly Bs – WATER WITCH

Water Witches are drawn to growing their psychic abilities and being in tune with you and others' emotional state.

Types of Water Witch include:

Sea Witch, River Witch, Bog Witch, Chalice Witch, Solitary Witch, Cosmic Witch, Communal Witch, Pact Witch, Storm Witch, Mental Witch, Liminal Witch, Empath Witch, Dream Witch, Astral Witch, Astrological Witch, Mermaid Witch, Love Witch, Lunar Witch, Psychopomp Witch, Tea Witch, Shadow Witch, Empath Witch, Psionic Witch, Still Witch, Travel Witch

Mostly Cs – AIR WITCH

Air Witches are drawn to powers of the mind and intellect. They are creative, playful and light-hearted.

Types of Air Witch include:

Fae Witch, Angur Witch, Pop-Culture Witch, Art Witch, Rhythmic Witch, Fashion Witch, Wand Witch, Personal-Space Witch, Sigil Witch, Trickster Witch, Angelic Witch, Smoke Witch, Color Witch, Ceremonial Witch, Solar Witch, Literary Witch, Illusion Witch, Deific Witch, Spirit Witch, Knit Witch, Paper Witch, Emanant Witch, Invocation Witch, Beauty Witch, Giddy Witch

Mostly Ds – EARTH WITCH

Earth Witches are drawn to gaining a deeper connection with nature and the treasures of the earth.

Types of Earth Witch include:

Ancestral Witch, Pentacle Witch, Crystal Witch, Hedge Witch, Kitchen Witch, Necromancy Witch, Green Witch, Medicinal Witch, Luck Witch, Familiar Witch, Traditional Witch, Nocturnal Witch, Cottage Witch, Garden Witch, Religious Witch, Metallurgy Witch, Flora Witch, Masonry Witch, Urban Witch, Farm Witch, Wild Witch, Root Witch, Poison Witch, Fortune Witch, Demolition Witch

curse
reversal

CURSE
REVERSAL

POTIONS

CURSE REVERSAL POTIONS

Have you been feeling off lately? Like everything you do goes wrong, everything you touch breaks and everything you say is misunderstood? If you believe you've become the victim of a curse, these potions will set things right.

There are some simple tests you can perform to determine whether or not you've been cursed. Coincidences that defy natural law are a key indicator that something isn't right. For example, flipping four coins will commonly result in 50 per cent of the coins landing on heads or tails. If you continually flip four coins and each time they land on the exact same side, this is a violation of natural law and a sign that things aren't quite right with your energies. Or if you crack an egg and see a bloody yolk or notice a large number of white clots in the egg white, it's an indicator of a blockage due to negative energy. Fret not, love, we've got some potions to set you right!

The simplest way to break a curse is to bathe in uncrossing herbs and sea salt. An easy recipe for a salt scrub is equal parts sea salt to olive oil that's been steeped with ground uncrossing herbs, then strained. Uncrossing herbs include angelica, mint, sandalwood, sage, rosemary, lemongrass, roses, John the Conqueror root and bay leaf.

Typically, uncrossing rituals are always performed for either three, seven, nine or 13 days. The ingredients used in these rituals also follow that same rule, with the number increasing based on severity.

This is your moment to blind the evil eye, remove any jinxes, uncross hexes placed upon you and banish that negative energy for good! Gulp down these brews to turn the energy of evil intent back on its source or reverse your own bad luck to adjust the scales in your favor.

For vegan substitutes please see page 28.

CORRESPONDENCES

INCENSE

basil, bay, coffee, patchouli, rosemary, rue, sage, sandalwood

CRYSTALS TO WORK WITH FOR CURSE REVERSAL SPELLS

black tourmaline, onyx, clear quartz, selenite

DAYS OF THE WEEK FOR CURSE REVERSAL SPELLS

Tuesday, Saturday, Sunday

PLANETS FOR CURSE REVERSAL SPELLS

Mars, Saturn, Sun

ZODIAC SIGNS FOR CURSE REVERSAL SPELLS

Aries, Scorpio, Capricorn

MOON PHASE FOR CURSE REVERSAL SPELLS

Waning Moon (but any time is a good time for curse reversal!)

HATER BLOCKER

As the saying goes, "The best defense is a good offense." And nothing will stop the haters in their tracks like some quality hater blockers, which simultaneously block the harmful rays of the Sun while also reflecting the deadly shade some people would throw your way, back on to them.

The best accompaniment to your badass ensemble is, of course, Hater Blocker in potion form, your drinkable ally in arms. Walk with your head held high, grasping your favorite reusable traveling cup filled to the brim with a healthy dose of "get the hell out my face!" and just keep on walking.

Oh, how the haters love to stare.

Key correspondence included in this drink:

STAR ANISE. Anise pods are used in magickal workings for clairvoyance, luck, spiritual offerings, protection, power generation, banishing evil, prophetic visions, clarity.

Note on drink preference: *This coffee-based potion should be made to suit your taste. If you prefer your coffee hot, ice, blended or turned into a latte with milk, it is up to you. It will not interfere with the potency of the potion. As long as you ensure the key correspondence and salt remains, it will remain magickally potent.*

INGREDIENTS

★ 4 tbsp whipping cream (or non-dairy alternative)

★ Black lava sea salt (or regular salt; you may also use the collective salt from your haters)

★ 240ml/8fl oz/ 1 cup strong black coffee with 6 star anise steeped within

★ 2 tbsp sweetener of your choice

Magickal Garnish

★ Sea salt

RITUAL

CARVE INTO A CANDLE: "ALL HARMFUL ENERGY CAST UNTO ME, RETURN IT TO ITS SOURCE, SO MOTE IT BE!", THEN LIGHT IT. HOLD A CUP IN BOTH HANDS, CONCENTRATING FOR 3 MINS ON IMBUING REFLECTIVE ENERGY, AND REPELLING ANY NEGATIVE ENERGIES. LEAVE YOUR CUP NEXT TO THE CANDLE, UNTIL IT BURNS DOWN.

METHOD

★ Whip the cream until slightly thickened, then stir in the sea salt and set aside.

★ Sweeten the coffee with your preferred sweetener.

★ Strain the anise-steeped coffee into your traveler cup and top with the salted whipped cream.

★ Sprinkle over a little extra sea salt and enjoy!

NOTE

Please never leave a lit candle unattended. You could have a stay-at-home detox weekend so you can keep watch over your candle and perform any additional cleansing/protection rituals.

CURSE REVERSAL POTIONS

ABOUT FACE

It's time to make that negative energy in the comment section do a 180. This citrus bomb is empowered by both grapefruit and orange, which both pack a powerful protective punch.

Whereas the previous potion is an offensive drinkable spell, this one uses the power of defensive magick. It's time to put your defensive powers to work for you and restore your sense of strength and security in your digital space.

Key correspondences included in this drink are:

GRAPEFRUIT. Grapefruit is associated with magickal workings involving grounding, stability, happiness, knowing your worth, legal matters, removing negativity from your life, and increasing your physical energy.

ORANGE. Orange is associated with magickal workings involving success in business, building confidence, courage, divination, employment, fertility, good luck, grounding and stability, removing negativity, increasing your physical energy, and promoting happiness and success in legal matters.

INGREDIENTS

★ 5 tbsp
   grapefruit juice
★ 5 tbsp orange
   juice
★ 5 tbsp lemon-
   lime soda
★ Ice cubes

Magickal Garnish
★ Citrus slices
   from lemon,
   lime, orange
   and/or
   grapefruit

RITUAL

BLOW UP A RED
BALLOON. IMAGINE
IT INFLATING WITH
ALL THE NEGATIVITY
YOU EXPERIENCE
ONLINE. ON ONE
SIDE WRITE ABOUT
WHY YOU FEEL
UNSAFE IN THAT
SPACE. ON THE
OTHER SIDE DRAW A
PERSONIFICATION
OF THE SOURCES
OF NEGATIVITY.
BEFORE DRINKING
YOUR POTION, POP
THE BALLOON,
OPEN A WINDOW
FOR THE AIR
TO REMOVE
THE NEGATIVITY,
AND THROW THE
BALLOON AWAY.

METHOD

★ To a tall serving glass filled with ice, add
the grapefruit juice and orange juice.

★ Pour in the lemon-lime soda.

★ Garnish with slices of lemon, lime,
orange and/or grapefruit. Stir, and enjoy!

CANCELED

Our emotions need protection just as much as anything else in our life. If you feel you've been neglecting your emotional health and wish to do some inner healing and protection work, then a sip from this potion will do just the trick. This brew comes with a one-two punch: you'll be receiving curse-reversal help through the ritual, and restorative powers through the potion itself – providing you with a dual whammy to rebalance your emotional state.

Key correspondence included in this drink:

HONEYDEW MELON (can be substituted for wintermelon or watermelon). Honeydew melons and melons in general are associated with fertility, beauty, youth, longevity and abundance. They have the power to generate love and happiness in relationships and can promote self-love.

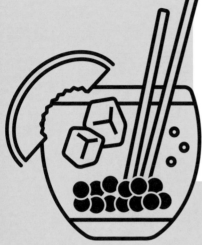

INGREDIENTS

- ★ 2 tbsp tapioca pearls/boba balls (optional)
- ★ 75g/2½oz/ ½ cup chopped honeydew melon flesh
- ★ Handful of ice cubes
- ★ A scoop of vanilla ice cream
- ★ 3½ tbsp Amoretti honeydew melon syrup
- ★ Milk or non-dairy alternative (optional)

Magickal Garnish
- ★ Slices of melon

RITUAL

PLACE A SMALL MIRROR INTO A BOWL OF BLACK SALT. PUT SOMETHING THAT REPRESENTS THE NEGATIVITY FACING THE MIRROR. THIS COULD BE A SIMPLE DRAWING. COVER THE BOWL WITH A DARK CLOTH TO ISOLATE AND SEVER THE NEGATIVITY FROM YOU WHILE YOU IMBIBE THE POTION. DISCARD THE BOWL WITHOUT LOOKING AT IT.

METHOD

- ★ If using tapioca pearls/boba balls, prepare them according to the packet.

- ★ Place the rest of the ingredients in a blender and blend for 30 secs until smooth. Add a little milk or milk substitute to thin the mixture if it's too thick.

- ★ Pour the potion into a serving glass containing the tapioca pearls, if using.

- ★ Garnish with melon slices and enjoy!

NOTE

It's common for witches to have a mundane trashcan for everyday use as well as a smaller one for magickal trash. Magickal trash contains discarded materials from magickal workings and is typically disposed of at a crossroads at least one mile away from your home.

POTIONS FOR

THE COVEN

POTIONS FOR THE COVEN

Who's ready for some coven lovin'? You might be a group of 13 or maybe it's just you and your better half. No matter the size of your coven, any time is a good time when they're by your side. Let's celebrate your magickal friendships with a toast, music that slaps and a cheer to keep the good times going!

Never underestimate the power of friendship. A deep comradery is the foundation of any coven and when you layer on laughs, trust and genuine love for one another, your squad becomes a force to be reckoned with. The reason there is such an enormous amount of power in groups is because the collective mind or hive mind allows coven members with shared beliefs to tap into powers greater than themselves. Also, when you have more than one person focusing on creating a change, it's likely to come about more swiftly.

The potions in this chapter are perfect for groups looking to transform an average night into a celebration filled with magickal fun. Send out that mass text invite to let your friends know it's going down during the witching hour, with a note to leave any bitchcraft at the door. Dim the lights, light a few dozen candles for a festive vibe and get ready to throw a witch's ball so bangin' the attendees will be spellbound.

For vegan substitutes please see page 28.

CORRESPONDENCES

INCENSE

acacia, allspice, angelica, bluebell, carnation, cinnamon, citronella, cloves, gardenia, lavender, lemon, linden, meadowsweet, myrtle, papaya, passion flower, rose, sweet pea

CRYSTALS TO WORK WITH FOR COVEN SPELLS

aventurine, blue lace agate, carnelian, emerald, garnet, green tourmaline, jade, lapis lazuli, peridot, rhodonite, rose quartz, ruby, selenite, snowflake obsidian, topaz, turquoise

DAY OF THE WEEK FOR COVEN SPELLS

Friday

PLANET FOR COVEN SPELLS

Venus

ZODIAC SIGNS FOR COVEN SPELLS

Leo, Scorpio, Sagittarius

MOON PHASE FOR COVEN SPELLS

Waxing Moon

HALLOQUEENS
& PUMPKINGS

★★ 🍸 🍁

Your time has come once again, my liege! When the air is crisp and the leaves begin to fall, everyone knows it is the season of your reign. Celebrate the glory that is your excellence, fair halloqueens and grand pumpkings! Let us toast to our spooky autumnal royal court.

Key correspondences included in this drink are:

PUMPKIN. Pumpkin is associated with spellwork involving granting wishes, love, prosperity and fertility, as well as protection if used to make a jack-o'-lantern.

PUMPKIN SPICE. Pumpkin spice is a blend of cinnamon, nutmeg, ginger, cloves and allspice. These spices have been used in magickal workings for success, sex, banishing illnesses, resolving conflicts, protection for or from the law, good luck, strength and courage, and victory in battles.

INGREDIENTS

Serves 4

- ★ 250ml/9fl oz/ 1 cup Baileys Pumpkin Spice
- ★ 8 scoops of pumpkin ice cream (or vanilla ice cream)
- ★ 125ml/4fl oz/ ½ cup whole milk/half and half (or non-dairy alternative)

- ★ 3 tbsp soft brown sugar
- ★ 2 tbsp pumpkin purée
- ★ 1 tbsp pumpkin spice

Magickal Garnish
- ★ Cinnamon sticks
- ★ Pumpkin spice

METHOD

★ Put all the ingredients into a blender and blend until smooth, about 1 min.

★ Pour into short serving glasses and top each with a cinnamon stick.

★ Garnish with a sprinkle of extra pumpkin spice and enjoy!

RITUAL

IMBUE THE PUMPKIN SPICE WITH INTENTIONS OF FRIENDSHIP AND FRIVOLITY BY HOLDING THE PUMPKIN SPICE CONTAINER IN BOTH HANDS, CLOSING YOUR EYES AND FOCUSING ON TAPPING INTO THE ENERGIES WITHIN TO BRING YOUR DESIRE INTO REALITY.

PINKETTY DRINKETTY

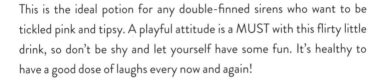

This is the ideal potion for any double-finned sirens who want to be tickled pink and tipsy. A playful attitude is a MUST with this flirty little drink, so don't be shy and let yourself have some fun. It's healthy to have a good dose of laughs every now and again!

Key correspondence included in this drink:

ACAI. Acai berries are associated with cleansing, desire, fire magick, healing, love, lust, physical energy, sex magick, sexuality and strength.

INGREDIENTS

Serves 4

- ★ 4 acai berry tea bags
- ★ 240ml/8fl oz/ 1 cup boiling water
- ★ 125ml/4fl oz/ ½ cup white grape juice
- ★ 90ml/3fl oz/ generous ⅓ cup vodka

- ★ Ice cubes
- ★ 500ml/17fl oz/ 2 cups coconut milk
- ★ 175ml/6fl oz/ ¾ cup sweetener of choice (optional)

Magickal Garnish
- ★ Sliced strawberries

METHOD

★ In a heatproof container, steep the tea bags in the hot water for 6 mins, then remove and discard them.

★ Pour the white grape juice and vodka into the tea.

★ Fill 4 serving glasses with ice and add about 120ml/4fl oz/½ cup of the tea mixture to each. Add sweetener to the desired sweetness and top off with coconut milk.

★ Garnish each glass with sliced strawberries before serving.

RITUAL

THIS FLIRTY AND FEMININE DRINK DESERVES ATTENTION OF EQUAL MEASURE. IT'S TIME TO PRACTICE YOUR WINK, COY SMILE AND COQUETTISH GIGGLE WITH ALL WHOM YOU GRACE WITH YOUR PRESENCE.

FROGS' BRAINS

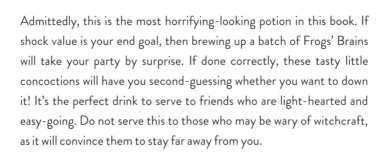

Admittedly, this is the most horrifying-looking potion in this book. If shock value is your end goal, then brewing up a batch of Frogs' Brains will take your party by surprise. If done correctly, these tasty little concoctions will have you second-guessing whether you want to down it! It's the perfect drink to serve to friends who are light-hearted and easy-going. Do not serve this to those who may be wary of witchcraft, as it will convince them to stay far away from you.

Key correspondence included in this drink:

BAILEYS IRISH CREAM. This cream liqueur is made with cream, cocoa, vanilla, coffee and whiskey, which corresponds to magickal workings related to protection, strength, energy, prosperity, love, healing, fertility, marriage and financial luck.

INGREDIENTS

★ 2 tbsp peach schnapps
★ 1 tbsp Baileys Irish Cream
★ 1 tbsp grenadine

RITUAL

CHANNEL YOUR
INNER CRONE
AND CACKLE
AS LOUDLY AS
POSSIBLE AFTER
DOWNING THIS
FROGS' BRAINS.

METHOD

★ First pour the peach schnapps into a
50ml/2fl oz shot glass.

★ Slowly pour in the Baileys Irish Cream
and allow it to float to the surface.

★ Finish off by gently pouring in the
grenadine. Drink and enjoy!

WITCH'S BREW

It's time to break out your largest cauldron and mix up a batch of Witch's Brew! This party-pleasing potion is perfect for large gatherings. The green hue, which comes from the Midori melon liqueur, is spooky and festive. If you want to take this potion over the top, all you'll need is some dry ice and creepy gummy garnishes.

Fair warning: beware the Witch's Brew, it bites back.

Key correspondences included in this drink are:

APPLE. Apples are associated with magickal workings involving passion, love, health and immortality.

CHERRY. Cherries have the power to aid in divination workings, induce sleep, induce dreams and promote healthy eyesight. They also act as an anti-inflammatory.

MELON. Melons in general are associated with fertility, beauty, youth, longevity and abundance. They have the power to generate love and happiness in relationships and can promote self-love. Melons can help in clearing energy blockages, unburdening your heart and releasing old pain.

INGREDIENTS Serves 6–8

- ★ 700ml/24fl oz/ 3 cups Midori melon liqueur
- ★ 300ml/10fl oz/ 1¼ cups light rum
- ★ 600ml/20fl oz/ 2½ cups white cranberry juice
- ★ 300ml/10fl oz/ 1¼ cups apple juice
- ★ 150ml/5fl oz/ scant ⅔ cup lemon-lime soda
- ★ Juice of 1 lime (or lemon)
- ★ 300ml/10fl oz/ 1¼ cups sweetener of your choice

Magickal Garnish
- ★ Blueberries
- ★ Honeydew melon balls
- ★ Cherries
- ★ Gummy worms

METHOD

★ Mix all the ingredients together in a large punch bowl.

★ Add the fruit garnishes and gummy candy of your choice.

★ Speak the incantation, then stir to activate the spell.

★ Divide between glasses and drink.

RITUAL

SPEAK ALOUD THIS INCANTATION, FILLING IN THE GAPS AS YOU WISH: "ALL WHO VENTURE TO THIS PLACE OF _____ BE WARNED, FOR ALL WHO ENTER MUST _____ OR BE FOREVER SCORNED! TOSS BACK THIS BREW YOU _____, I SAY DRINK UP! AND ALL NIGHT LONG YOU'LL RUSH TO REFILL THY CUP!"

JU JU JUNGLE JUICE

This alluring potion will entrance all who gaze upon it and put the drinker under its spell. If you've ever wanted the power to bewitch the mind and ensnare the senses (yes, that is a Harry Potter reference), give this potion your undivided attention.

Magickal moments can be manufactured by those ingenious enough to put particular puzzle pieces in the right place. Allow this brew to work an entire room just for you. With this one potion, the power of an unforgettable party is close at hand.

Key correspondences included in this drink are:

APPLE. Apples are associated with magickal workings involving passion, love, health and immortality.

FIREBALL WHISKEY. This cinnamon-flavored whiskey has correspondences associated with protection, strength, vigor, sexuality, lust, love, fertility, good luck, growth, transformation and energy.

INGREDIENTS

Serves 4

★ 350ml/12fl oz/ scant 1½ cups natural apple juice/apple cider

★ 350ml/12fl oz/ scant 1½ cups cranberry juice

★ 100ml/3½fl oz/ scant ½ cup Fireball whiskey

★ 4 tbsp grenadine

★ 1 tsp edible gold glitter

★ Ice cubes

RITUAL

AS YOU SPRINKLE IN THE EDIBLE GLITTER, IMAGINE THAT ALL WHO DRINK THIS POTION WILL FEEL ENCHANTED AND DAZZLED BY THE PEOPLE AROUND THEM AND THE NIGHT'S EVENTS.

METHOD

★ Combine all the ingredients in a jug/ pitcher filled with ice.

★ Stir to combine, then pour into serving glasses filled with ice.

★ Enjoy!

INDEX